FINANCE FOR BUSINESS

A Guide for the Lending Banker

FINANCE FOR BUSINESS

A Guide for the Lending Banker

Keith Checkley FCIB

Financial Training

First published in Great Britain 1988 by Financial Training Publications Limited, Holland House, 140-144 Freston Road, London W10 6TR

ISBN: 1 85185 069 4

Typeset by LKM Typesetting Ltd, London EC1
Printed by Dotesios Printers Ltd, Bradford-upon-Avon, Wilts

Contents

Preface

The competitive environment for businesses has changed greatly in recent years. The success of any business will always depend upon the skill, knowledge and tenacity of those running the firm.

Business management and finance still cause the most problems for the smaller business. Bankers can help with an understanding of finance to assist business development.

This book has been written principally for banking students, and bank managers 'at the sharp end'. The principles outlined will apply to any business, whether new or existing, where the value of stock and cash flow relate to the cycle of production.

I hope you will enjoy reading this book and it will help you in your approach to your business customer.

Keith Checkley

ACKNOWLEDGEMENTS

I am grateful to *The Investors Chronicle*, The Government Statistics and Market Intelligence Library, The Bank of England Industrial Finance Division, The Department of Trade and Industry, Bank Information Services and The Chartered Institute of Bankers for their help in providing statistics and information.

My thanks are also due to Keith Dickinson, Phil Fielding, Mike Hill and my sister Sheila.

Finally, I should like to thank the directors and staff of Financial Training Publications Limited, for without their support and enthusiasm this project would not have taken place.

Part One

Business organisation

1 The business scene

INTRODUCTION

The telephone rings — your secretary says, 'Excuse me; I have Mr Businessman on the line — he would like an appointment to see you.'

How do you feel about this? If it's your first business interview you could be fairly apprehensive! It will certainly be different from any *personal* lending interview that you may have conducted.

A number of questions may spring to mind:

* What type of business is it likely to be — sole trader — company — partnership?

* Will you use the same analysis techniques?

* If it is a start-up business, how can you assess the risk?

* What capital gearing level are you prepared to consider?

To enable you to answer these and other questions, we shall be considering, in Part One, the general organisation of businesses. In Part Two we shall look at assessing the lending proposition. And lastly, Part Three will deal with the various types of financial support for businesses.

Figure 1 The business scene

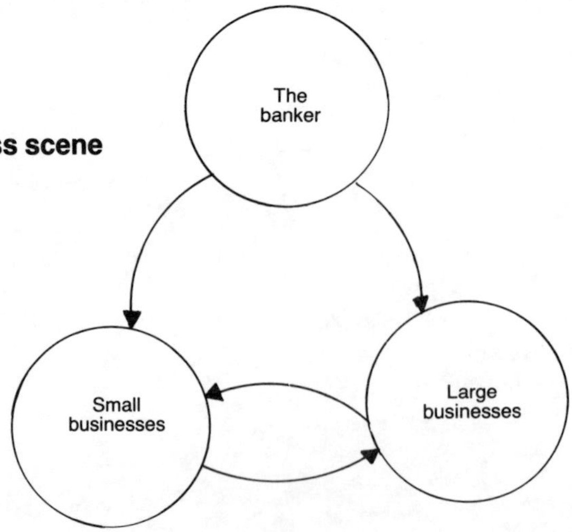

BANKS AND THEIR BUSINESS ACCOUNTS

The UK clearing banks have over 11,000 branches dealing with in excess of 35 million account holders. We can quickly reduce this overall number to the business accounts which we handle by reviewing some data from The Government Statistics and Market Intelligence Library.

Recent figures of businesses totalled 1.4 million units, split as follows:

Table 1

Trade classification	Number of units, 1982 (000)
Agriculture	164
Production	152
Construction	202
Road transport and transport services	59
Wholesaling and dealing	111
Retailing	267
Finance, property and professional services	96
Catering	119
Motor trades	74
Other services	156
Total	1,400

SIZE OF BUSINESS

Furthermore, the 'size' of these businesses is significant. Additional analysis by using turnover size bands reveals that over 90 per cent of businesses had a turnover of less than £1 million (see Table 2).

Table 2 Analysis of business by turnover size

Trade classification	Turnover band (£000) 0-16	17-49	50-99	100-249
Agriculture	56,718 (35)	55,337 (34)	27,742 (17)	17,696 (11)
Mining and quarrying and public utilities	419 (23)	220 (12)	207 (12)	301 (17)
Manufacturing industries	24,887 (17)	34,619 (23)	23,336 (16)	27,066 (18)
Food, drink and tobacco	1,059 (11)	1,813 (19)	1,733 (18)	1,828 (19)
Coal and petroleum products	28 (12)	28 (12)	26 (11)	39 (16)
Chemicals and allied industries	613 (15)	607 (15)	454 (11)	673 (16)
Metal manufacture	306 (10)	508 (17)	368 (12)	533 (18)
Mechanical engineering	4,262 (17)	5,909 (23)	3,943 (15)	4,780 (19)
Instrument engineering	637 (20)	685 (22)	452 (15)	528 (17)
Electrical engineering	2,027 (20)	2,265 (22)	1,395 (14)	1,671 (16)
Shipbuilding and marine engineering	522 (23)	540 (24)	326 (14)	366 (16)
Vehicles	209 (13)	231 (15)	160 (10)	221 (14)
Metal goods not elsewhere specified	2,811 (16)	4,129 (23)	2,743 (16)	3,454 (20)
Textiles	880 (13)	1,179 (18)	885 (14)	1,116 (17)
Leather, leather goods and fur	314 (15)	523 (26)	338 (17)	378 (19)
Clothing and footwear	1,374 (12)	2,828 (25)	2,346 (21)	2,257 (20)
Bricks, pottery, glass, cement, etc.	513 (17)	639 (21)	393 (13)	434 (15)
Timber, furniture, etc.	2,539 (19)	3,690 (28)	1,909 (14)	2,133 (16)
Paper, printing and publishing	4,132 (18)	5,738 (26)	3,626 (16)	4,025 (18)
Other manufacturing industries	2,661 (18)	3,307 (23)	2,239 (15)	2,630 (18)
Construction	58,067 (29)	75,204 (37)	27,871 (14)	22,532 (11)
Road transport and transport services	13,287 (22)	22,991 (39)	7,601 (13)	7,288 (12)
Wholesaling and dealing	16,039 (15)	22,783 (21)	17,234 (16)	21,171 (19)
Retailing	26,714 (10)	100,376 (38)	74,048 (28)	48,231 (18)
Finance, property and professional services	32,256 (34)	30,165 (32)	11,520 (12)	11,091 (12)
Catering	9,684 (8)	51,876 (44)	36,192 (30)	16,932 (14)
Motor trades	11,135 (15)	21,535 (29)	11,317 (15)	13,008 (18)
Other services	46,323 (30)	60,482 (39)	20,111 (13)	15,575 (10)
Total	295,529 (21)	475,588 (34)	257,179 (18)	200,891 (14)

Source: The Government Statistics and Market Intelligence Library

Table 2

250-499		500-999		1,000-4,999		5,000 and over		Total
4,287	(3)	1,530	(1)	621	(—)	86	(—)	164,017
171	(10)	137	(8)	195	(11)	139	(8)	1,789
14,166	(9)	10,060	(7)	11,761	(8)	4,557	(3)	150,452
923	(10)	615	(6)	990	(10)	695	(7)	9,656
21	(9)	24	(10)	41	(17)	35	(14)	242
447	(11)	403	(10)	593	(14)	395	(9)	4,185
332	(1)	290	(10)	435	(14)	259	(9)	3,031
2,524	(10)	1,731	(7)	1,890	(7)	663	(3)	25,702
272	(9)	224	(7)	257	(8)	61	(2)	3,116
905	(9)	650	(6)	829	(8)	415	(4)	10,157
187	(8)	119	(5)	156	(7)	62	(3)	2,278
167	(11)	165	(11)	238	(15)	158	(10)	1,549
1,778	(10)	1,148	(7)	1,203	(7)	315	(2)	17,581
703	(11)	662	(10)	840	(13)	285	(4)	6,550
198	(10)	106	(5)	156	(8)	23	(1)	2,036
888	(8)	636	(6)	663	(6)	153	(1)	11,145
290	(10)	223	(7)	345	(12)	152	(5)	2,989
1,149	(9)	790	(6)	841	(6)	185	(1)	13,236
1,984	(6)	1,261	(6)	1,228	(5)	407	(2)	22,401
1,398	(10)	1,013	(7)	1,056	(7)	294	(2)	14,598
8,935	(4)	4,866	(2)	3,730	(2)	894	(—)	202,099
3,574	(6)	2,201	(4)	1,903	(3)	416	(1)	59,261
11,914	(11)	9,006	(8)	9,879	(9)	2,477	(2)	110,503
10,583	(4)	3,860	(1)	2,167	(1)	626	(—)	266,605
4,319	(5)	2,479	(3)	2,370	(2)	1,392	(1)	95,592
2,903	(2)	846	(1)	478	(—)	107	(—)	119,018
7,076	(10)	4,930	(7)	4,189	(6)	740	(1)	73,930
5,631	(4)	3,235	(2)	3,198	(2)	1,363	(1)	155,918
73,559	(5)	43,150	(3)	40,491	(3)	12,797	(1)	1,399,184

You can see, therefore, that many businesses you will be asked to finance are likely to be classified as 'small'.

TYPE OF BUSINESS

Businesses can be broken down as follows:

Sole proprietorships	561,246
Partnerships	370,737
Corporate	515,840
Total	1,447,823

Source: The Government Statistics and Market Intelligence Library, 1982.

From these figures you will see that sole proprietorship is the most popular trading format, at 561,246 units, with corporate businesses a close second.

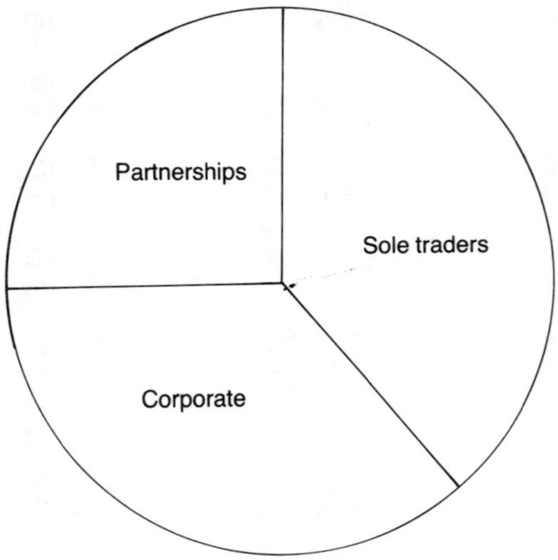

Figure 2 Type of business (units)

In chapter 7 we will consider the 'weighting' of lending risk according to business structure.

THE BOLTON REPORT

Since you are most likely to encounter a 'small' business, we shall now consider the first major study of small businesses, which was published in 1971. This *Report of the Committee of Inquiry on Small Firms* was chaired by J. E. Bolton. Many significant points were made in the report as to the structure and financial needs of small businesses.

The Bolton Report (as it is commonly known) found that defining a small business was difficult, in that employment of assets, turnover, output, employees or whatever measure used, might not be applicable to each and every sector of small businesses. However, an adoption had to be made for each sector and was as shown in Table 3.

Table 3 Small firm sector as defined by the Bolton Committee

Industry classification	Statistical definition of small firms used by the Committee	Small firms (as defined as a % of all firms in the industry) 1962	Average employment per small firm 1963
Manufacturing	200 employees or less	94	25
Retailing	Turnover £50,000 p.a. or less (1963 prices)	96	3
Wholesale trades	Turnover £200,000 p.a. or less (1963 prices)	77	7
Construction	25 employees or less	89	6
Mining/quarrying	25 employees or less	77	11
Motor trades	Turnover £100,000 p.a. or less (1963 prices)	87	3
Miscellaneous services	Turnover £50,000 p.a. or less (1963 prices)	90	4
Road transport	5 vehicles or less	85	4
Catering	All except multiples and brewery-managed public houses	96	3

It is worth mentioning the high percentage figures revealed but the low number of average employees. In formulating these sector definitions the Committee of Inquiry had the following business characteristics in mind:

(a) In economic terms, a small firm is one that has a relatively small share of its market.

(b) An essential characteristic of a small firm is that it is managed by its owners in a personalised way.

(c) It is independent in the sense that it does not form part of a larger enterprise which can provide a financial umbrella.

(d) The owner-managers should be free from outside control in taking their principal decisions.

The turnover bands shown in Table 2 are now of course way out of date due to inflationary trends. Perhaps a broad definition of a small business that would be acceptable is: ‘a small business is one employing less than 200 people and having an annual turnover of less than £3 million’.

Importance of the small business sector

The Bolton Report indicated the principal functions of the sector as:

(a) Providing outlets for large numbers of individualistic people who preferred to work in small units.

(b) Providing an essential source of suppliers to large firms.

(c) Performing a highly economic role in those areas where a large variety of products and where customer service was of key importance.

(d) Providing variety of choice for the consumer.

(e) Contributing towards a balanced and stable industrial structure.

(f) Offering an essential source of innovation, and a seed-bed for large firms of the future.

(g) Furnishing a source of entirely new industries.

(h) Maintaining a means of entry to business for new entrepreneurial talent.

Some Bolton Report conclusions

* Ample information is readily available about sources of finance, but surprisingly enough there does seem to be an ‘information gap’. Although small firms suffer a number of genuine disabilities by comparison with large firms in seeking finance from external sources, most of these disabilities reflect the higher costs of lending in small amounts or the higher risk of lending to small borrowers. They do not result from imperfections in the supply of finance — indeed, the ability and readiness of the financial institutions to exploit every new legitimate demand for funds is one of the greatest strengths of our financial system. Some 93 per cent of small firms approached the clearing banks as their only source of external finance.

* What is required above all for the health of the small firm sector is an economic and taxation system which will enable individuals to acquire or establish new businesses out of personal resources and to develop these on the base of retained profits. Without this no institutional financing arrangements can preserve the small firm sector.

* Bolton’s question: ‘If you need help, to which of the following would you be most likely to turn?’ was answered by 3,740 firms as follows:

Accountant	1,383
Solicitor	561
Bank manager	543
Chamber of Commerce	496
Trade association	485
Business consultant	143
CBI	129

Bolton concluded that the main areas in which small businesses could improve their performances were:

(a) *Finance* Small firms frequently lack knowledge of the appropriate sources of development finance and working capital. They are also unskilled in presenting a financial case to potential investors and lenders.

(b) *Costing and control information* Cost control is often so poor that management frequently learns of an impending crisis only with the appearance of annual accounts or following an urgent call from the bank manager. Credit control and stock control information is often inadequate.

(c) Other reasons of weakness were organisation, marketing, information use and retrieval, personnel management, technological change, production scheduling and purchase control.

Bolton went on to suggest that if it were possible for the banks to impose as a normal condition for the grant of an overdraft to a firm, the production of regular cash flow statements, or the employment of adequate estimating and budgetary systems (including age lists of debtors and an analysis of stocks in relation to future production programmes), and if such disciplines came to be recognised as helpful for obtaining bank finance, the efficiency of small firms might be increased.

Hence, the bank manager might be able to improve the efficiency of his customers, in their interests and his own. He could help them by pointing out the benefits of regular attention to certain simple indices of the health of a business — the profit/sales ratio, the stocks/turnover ratio, return on capital and so on.

2 Why small businesses fail

Bankers may recall that in November 1982 chartered accountants Robson Rhodes reported on the circumstances giving rise to the first 50 claims made on the Department of Industry in respect of failed businesses under the Small Business Loan Guarantee Scheme. Robson Rhodes were appointed by the Secretary of State for Industry to report on a range of matters as required by the Department of Industry Economics Division.

Robson Rhodes were able to study 48 of the 50 cases, as in two cases it proved impossible to gain access to the necessary information file. It is only fair to point out that the survey studied only failures and not successes — it would need a much wider survey before comment could be made on the Loan Guarantee Scheme as a whole.

THE SMALL BUSINESS LOAN GUARANTEE SCHEME (SBLGS)

Introduction

Under arrangements announced by the Chancellor of the Exchequer on 10 March 1981, small businesses in England, Scotland and Wales may be eligible for a loan guarantee by the Secretary of State for Trade and Industry under section 8 of the Industry Act 1972. In suitable cases, the Secretary of State will be prepared to guarantee repayment of 70 per cent of medium-term loans (not overdrafts) made by the English and Scottish clearing banks and Industrial and Commercial Finance Corporation (ICFC) to eligible small businesses for business purposes only. In consideration for this guarantee the Department of Industry will charge a commercial premium payable quarterly.

Eligibility

Applications for loans under the scheme, which should be made to one of the participating financial institutions, may be from sole traders, partnerships, cooperatives or limited companies. They may be already trading or they may be starting in business. There is no formal limitation based on numbers employed, turnover, assets, etc., but applications will not be considered from large businesses or their subsidiaries. Most sectors of the economy involving tradable goods and services are covered but there are some areas which are excluded.

Excluded activities

Agriculture and horticulture
Banking, finance and associated services
Commission agents (units primarily engaged in acting as intermediaries between buyer and seller and in carrying out transactions for the principal's account)
Education (including driving and flying schools providing training for non-commercial purposes)
Forestry (except tree harvesting and saw milling)
House and estate agents
Insurance and associates services
Medical and health services, veterinary services
Nightclubs and licensed clubs
Owning and dealing in real estate
Postal services and telecommunications
Public administration, national defence and compulsory social security
Railways
Recreational services and other cultural services
Tied public houses and bars
Travel agents

Further clarification may be obtained from the Department of Industry's Loan Guarantee Unit.

Amount and duration of loans

Guaranteed loans may be for amounts of up to £75,000 repayable over periods of between two and seven years.

Interest rates and other bank charges

The interest rate appropriate to individual guarantee loans will be decided by the lender, who will also charge an arrangement fee in accordance with his usual practice. The government's guarantee will reduce the risk borne by the lender, who will take this into account when deciding the interest rate appropriate to individual cases.

Premiums

The Department of Industry will charge a premium, usually 2½ per cent of the guaranteed amount (i.e., 70 per cent of the loan). The premium will reduce as the loan is repaid. Arrangements will be made for the premium to be paid quarterly in advance by direct debit.

Security

Applicants must be prepared to pledge all available assets used, or available for use, in connection with the business as security for guaranteed loans. This will not necessarily exclude from the scheme cases where such assets are not available.

Appraisal of applications

The primary appraisal of applications for guaranteed loans will be carried out by the lender, who must be satisfied that the proposition is viable, and is not one that he can sanction without the guarantee, before he can forward an application to the Department of Industry.

ANALYSIS OF THE FAILURES

Table 1 analyses the 48 failures, between new and existing businesses, between start-ups, buy-outs, lending for expansion or to businesses in urgent need. Those existing businesses which were in urgent need are classified as being 'in distress'. The statistics indicate that in failures two-thirds of the loans were to existing businesses. Table 2 further elaborates, highlighting the fact that half the businesses defined as 'existing' had been in existence less than 12 months prior to the application for a Scheme loan.

Table 1 Analysis of failures between new and existing businesses

		%
New businesses		
Start-up	11	22.9
Buy-out	5	10.4
	16	33.3
Existing businesses		
Expansion	14	29.2
Urgent need ('in distress')	18	37.5
	32	66.7
Total	48	

Table 2 Duration of existing business before application to LGS

Up to:	
6 months	8
12 months	8
	—
	16 (50%)
	—
2 years	7
3 years	4
More than 3 years	5
	—
	32
	—
Minimum	6 weeks
Maximum	12 years

Other significant facts to emerge were:

* 62% of the businesses failed within six months of receiving the Scheme loan. Small businesses often succeed or fail in what they are trying to do in a very short time.

* The shortest period of life was in fact a matter of days.

* The loan failures varied between £5,000 and £75,000.

* The average loan amount was £30,270 and the 50 failures totalled £1.5 million approximately.

Table 3 Activity analysis

	New	Existing	Total
Manufacturing			
General	0	1	1
Capital goods	0	6	6
Household goods	4	10	14
Food	0	0	0
Processing	2	0	2
Packaging products	0	3	3
	6	20	26 (54.2%)
Construction	1	0	1
Dealers, merchants and distributors	0	1	1
Printing and publishing	5	0	5
Retailing	2	3	5
Industrial services	0	4	4
General services, maintenance	0	2	2
Office services	1	0	1
House and personal services	1	2	3
Total	16	32	48

This table shows that 54.2 per cent of the failures were in manufacturing or were hoping to manufacture! You may draw your own conclusions from this.

Table 4 Reasons for failure

Market for product not as envisaged:	
Forecasts unrealistic	3
Forecasts optimistic but possible	5
Market decline	4
	12
Reasonable market, but poor management:	
Personal problems*	8
Poor management*	5
Lack of financial control	3
Poor marketing	4
Business neglected	1
	21
Other:	
Production problems	7
Competition	4
Deception	2
Loss of major customer	1
Overtrading	1
	15
	48

*These two overlap.

It is interesting to note from Table 4 that poor management was the cause of most failures. Also production problems and forecasts were both notable factors.

Robson Rhodes looked to four basic business skills when assessing each case — marketing, production, finance and purchasing — and invariably management was deficient in one or more of these skills.

Table 5 Was practical management advice taken from outsiders?

Bank	3
Accountant	6
Financial institution	1
Non-executive board member	2
Someone else	4
	—
	16
No one	36
	—
	52
	—

The table shows that 36 (70%) of the failures took no advice at all!

The survey revealed that a material number of businesses had such a high break-even level that the forecast results would be virtually impossible to achieve.

Table 6 % of sales forecast required to break-even

Up to 50%	3
50% to 60%	1
60% to 70%	6
	—
	10
70% to 80%	3
80% to 90%	10
90% to 100%	5
Over 100%	2
	—
	30
Details not known	18
	—
	48
	—

This table shows 20 per cent of businesses had a reasonable level to break even (up to 70%). However, in 37 per cent of all cases the details were not known, and a significant number required a high break-even level of sales.

Table 7 Was management information prepared?

Prepared:	
Copies not supplied to bank	6
Copies supplied to bank	13
	—
	19
Not prepared	29 (60.4%)
	—
	48
	—

It seems, therefore, that time taken to put in simple but sound bookkeeping routines and management information systems is time well spent.

Furthermore, *monitoring of progress is vital*, as shown by Table 8.

Table 8 Management information available for control of business

Projection of income and expenditure	
Yes	28
No	19 (40.4%)
Projection of cash flow	
Yes	47 (100%)*
No	—
Monthly statement of income	
Yes	6
No	41 (87.2%)
Monthly cash flow	
Yes	2
No	45 (95.7%)

*Table 8 totals only 47 businesses as the remaining 3 could not provide data.

Table 9 Initial capital gearing

Up to 1:1	3
1:1 to 2:1	7
2:1 to 3:1	3
3:1 to 5:1	4
5:1 to 10:1	2
10:1 to 20:1	1
Over 20:1	26
Information not available	2
	48

Over half the businesses had adverse gearing of over 20:1!

Robson Rhodes concluded that it would seem probable that any start-ups geared more than 5:1 should either benefit from some very unusual prospects or would need the closest attention in their early days.

High break-even, high gearing and low margins make a business very vulnerable to any adversity.

MANAGEMENT EXPERIENCE

Again accepting the limitation of the survey it is most revealing to look at the lack of experience in key areas.

Table 10 Was there previous experience in the following areas?

Marketing	
Yes	27
No	21 (43.7%)
	48
Production	
Yes	29
No	11 (22.9%)
Information not available	1
Not applicable	7
	48
Finance	
Yes	17
No	29 (60.4%)
Information not available	2
	48
Purchasing	
Yes	20
No	21 (43.7%)
Information not available	2
Not applicable	5
	48

BIRTHS AND DEATHS OF FIRMS IN THE UK

Having studied failures in detail you will be pleased to learn that overall there are more new businesses ('births') than 'deaths'.

The Department of Industry have produced provisional figures to show the trends over 1980-82 (Table 11).

Table 11 Provisional estimates for 1980-82: Births and deaths of firms by sector in the UK

Year	Trend	Agriculture	Production	Construction	Transport
1980 revised	Births	5,200	10,300	17,500	4,800
	Deaths	5,200	10,200	14,900	5,900
	Surplus	—	100	2,600	1,100
1981 provisional	Births	5,500	12,300	18,200	5,200
	Deaths	4,500	10,100	12,800	5,300
	Surplus	1,000	2,100	5,400	−100
1982 provisional	Births	2,900	13,700	17,800	5,900
	Deaths	4,500	11,100	14,400	5,200
	Surplus	−1,600	2,600	3,400	700
1980-82 provisional	Births	13,600	36,300	53,500	15,900
	Deaths	14,200	31,400	42,100	16,400
	Surplus	−600	4,800	11,400	−500

This table illustrates more births than deaths in 1981 and 1982 (+ 14,800 and + 7,000) as compared with a deficit of 2,000 in 1980.

Overall, 1980-82 there were	363,100	births
	343,100	deaths
resulting in a net gain of	19,800	

Table 11

Wholesale	Retail	Finance, property & professional services	Catering	Motor trades	Other services	Total
10,200	23,200	7,500	11,400	6,100	17,100	113,300
8,400	31,000	5,700	13,100	6,500	14,400	115,300
1,800	−7,800	1,800	−1,700	−400	2,700	−2,000
11,600	27,000	7,300	12,000	7,200	18,600	124,800
8,200	30,800	5,700	13,100	6,100	13,400	110,000
3,400	−3,900	1,600	−1,100	1,100	5,200	14,800
12,100	26,600	6,700	12,400	7,600	19,200	125,000
9,600	30,600	6,500	12,900	6,900	16,300	118,000
2,500	−4,000	200	−500	700	2,900	7,000
33,900	76,800	21,500	35,800	20,900	54,900	363,100
26,200	92,400	17,900	39,100	19,500	44,100	343,300
7,700	−15,700	3,600	−3,300	1,400	10,800	19,800

The sectors showing deficits over each of the three years were retailing and catering.

Table 12 Companies registered in Great Britain in 1982 and 1983

	1982		1983	
	Number	Nominal capital (£000)	Number	Nominal capital (£000)
Jan	4,122	45,549	6,224	63,513
Feb	7,698	119,474	7,410	175,932
Mar	8,645	141,787	8,849	98,719
Apr	6,728	94,528	8,412	134,030
May	6,566	52,616		
Jun	8,800	93,492		
Jul	8,147	214,276		
Aug	5,599	59,282		
Sep	7,660	226,138		
Oct	6,366	88,553		
Nov	8,413	117,791		
Dec	6,912	133,466		
Total	85,656	1,386,952		

Source: The Department of Trade and Industry.

Table 12 again confirms our 'small' business theme with an average nominal capital of only £16 per business registered during 1982.

CONCLUSION

Most businesses you as a banker will deal with will be small, or certainly at the 'smaller' end of the business scene.

Many will lack sophistication in financial skills. We will examine business strategy, financial planning and control in the next three chapters.

3 Business strategy

Financial planning has become more and more important over recent years due to the increasing competitiveness in the market place *whatever the product*, and also due to the rise in business costs particularly rent and wages. Businesses and bankers are becoming more aware of the need to improve planning to utilise the business resources to the maximum.

Where does finance fit in? The overall objectives of the business will dictate the business technical plan (or production plan), which in turn will require financing.

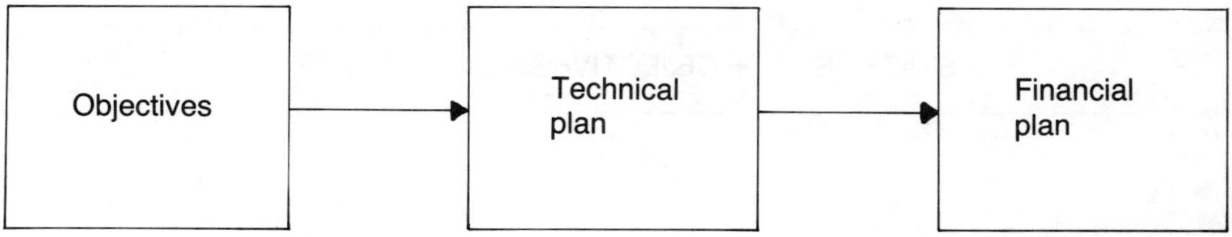

Figure 1 Development of business strategy

What type of questions should we ask business persons as they consider:

(a) their objectives;
(b) their business technical plan;
(c) their financial plan?

BUSINESS OBJECTIVES

Questions

* Have you developed clear objectives both short and long term?

* Are these objectives quantified in terms of market share, growth, product mix and rate of return?

* Have you built in review periods for your objectives and can you be flexible?

* Have you developed financial and technical plans from these objectives?

* Are your objectives realistic?
* Don't forget high turnover is not necessarily the final answer. Are you profitable?
* Have you considered the significance of your objectives relative to your capital base?
* Have you analysed both the strengths *and* weaknesses of your business?
* Have you analysed management expertise?
* Have you defined the limiting factors to your business?
* Have you *formulated* these objectives?

Formulating objectives

Below are three examples of ways of presenting objectives clearly on paper.

STATEMENT OF OBJECTIVES AND STRATEGY
1. To extend . . . .
2. To establish . . . .
3. To develop . . . .
4. etc.
5. etc.

Example 1

STATEMENT OF MEDIUM-TERM OBJECTIVES		
	Review dates	
Within the framework of our objectives our medium-term strategy is:		
1. To establish	x	x
2. To develop	x	x
3. etc.	x	x
4. etc.	x	x

Example 2

STATEMENT OF SHORT-TERM PLAN (12 MONTHS) AND ACTION	
Plan	*Action to be taken*
1. To develop	1. x x Responsibility:
2. To establish	2. x x Responsibility:
etc.	
etc.	

Example 3

Advantage of setting objectives

The advantages of setting such corporate objectives include:

* clarification of objectives
* establishing a link between strategy and action plans
* providing a framework for management/department action
* creating an involvement for management by setting objectives and accountability
* creating a motivating tool

THE TECHNICAL PLAN

This will consist of:

(a) management responsibilities and organisation;
(b) product monitoring/production and sales planning;
(c) efficiency controls.

Management responsibilities and organisation

Questions

* Do you have an organisational chart?
* Are there gaps in key areas of management, general management, sales, production, finance and personnel?
* Do you have recruitment, training and promotion plans?
* Can your management team cope with expansion of the business?
* Is each job clearly defined?
* Have you delegated routine tasks as far as possible?
* Are management accountable for specific areas of responsibility?
* Are there clearly defined lines of reporting?
* Do you coordinate projects with a team responsibility?

As we learned from the Bolton Report and the Robson Rhodes survey, good management is of vital importance.

In a start-up situation, quite often the proprietor will be sales or technically orientated. It is important that he or she acquires accountancy/financial know-how. Alternatively, he or she may build up a team which includes such specialised skills.

Obviously the larger the business, the more complex planning will become. An initial 'team' with expertise in the management of finance, sales, technology and accounts may not have sufficient depth if sales turnover grows into millions of pounds. Various areas of activity will need to be considered, such as personnel records, recruitment, selection, training, appraisal, career planning and management succession.

The business/corporate objectives discussed earlier will affect personnel planning both current and future. Management of departmental staffs must be aware of the need for accountability as a development of the business objectives.

Product marketing/production and sales planning

Questions

* Have you established the main factors affecting demand for your products, for example, market competition, prices, quantity, seasonality trends?
* Are your product lines expanding?
* Do you plan and research for follow-on products?
* Do you have a well-spread customer base?
* Do you monitor sales/goods returned as defective?
* Do you review 'make' or 'buy in' decisions?
* Have you defined specific sales areas and set sales targets?

Developing a marketing plan and committing this to paper in quantifiable terms is an essential follow-on from the business objectives we looked at earlier. By producing a plan containing targets for achievement within a coming period (usually 12 months), a standard is set against which performance can be measured.

In studying the market-place the business will benefit from an appraisal including market competition and market needs. Looking at existing products will help management to perceive the pattern of sales, as well as possible new product development to follow on from existing products.

Promotion of products can be carried out in different ways:

* media advertising
* the promotional package
* field personnel
* direct mail
* telephone sales

In order to monitor cost-effectiveness, a promotional budget should be set up and the ratio of costs to sales generated should be monitored.

Production operations planning

Questions

* Do you plan production levels to link in with exports and sales?

* If sales are made from finished goods stock, do you control lead-times correctly?

* Does your business have the physical production capability to meet planned sales?

* Are the premises adequate?

* Do you have job cards setting out raw material requirements and estimating labour/machine hours for specific products?

* Do you plan for effective production runs rather than piece-work?

* Do you monitor labour efficiency?

* Does your production controller liaise with your buyer to ensure an adequate, but not excessive, raw material stock?

* Do you monitor wastage of materials?

* Do you monitor defective goods returned?

Managing production is concerned with managing the physical resources of the business as efficiently as possible to create the products necessary to meet the marketing demand.

Production efficiency is *very* important. A high proportion of a manufacturing business's costs will be tied into production, for example:

* direct wages
* materials
* shop-floor machinery (capital costs and running costs)

No matter how well a job is estimated on a cost-of-materials and work-hours basis, if the production in terms of labour/materials usage efficiency is poor, then the *true* cost of the finished articles will be off budget.

Production can be thought of as the management of:

* design/layout of production
* scheduling and controlling of production
* labour management
* materials management
* quality control

'Make or buy' decisions will need to be made on a number of items and generally the decision will be on a cost-effective basis.

Efficiency controls

Key areas for consideration are:

(a) labour costs;
(b) stock control/purchase control;
(c) overheads control/analysis.

Labour efficiency

The paperwork for this can vary but usually involves:

* an identification slip for each job
* a progress document/card which moves and schedules progress
* materials/requisition order
* job instructions
* job booking for time spent/materials used

See examples 4 to 9.

Whether the papers are manual or computer-prepared does not matter. The prime consideration is simplicity. The job must be monitored for costs and labour/materials usage.

TIME SHEET

WEEK ENDING . . . . NAME. . . . .

DAY	JOB NO.	DESCRIPTION	START	STOP	HOURS
Monday					
Tuesday					
Wednesday					
Thursday					
Friday					
Saturday					
Sunday					

Example 4

LABOUR EFFICIENCY REPORT			
BY DEPARTMENT	WEEK ENDED.		
DEPARTMENT	PRODUCTION HOURS	BUDGETED HOURS	EFFICIENCY (%)
TOTALS			

Example 5

LABOUR EFFICIENCY REPORT			
BY JOB	WEEK ENDED.		
JOB NO.	PRODUCTION HOURS	BUDGETED HOURS	EFFICIENCY (%)
TOTALS			

Example 6

LABOUR ANALYSIS			
OVERALL COST BY DEPARTMENT		WEEK ENDED.	
DEPARTMENT	NO. OF EMPLOYEES	LABOUR COSTS	
		TOTAL	BUDGET
TOTALS			

Example 7

REFERENCE:

DATE:

O/No.

Detail:

Completion Date:

Example 8 'T' card or job scheduling card

ORDER FORM

ORDER WK. SHEET NO.

COMPANY NAME . . . . CUST. ORDER NO. . . . .
ADDRESS . . . . DATE . . . .
CONTACT NAME & TITLE . . . . TEL. NO. . . . .

ITEM	DESCRIPTION	DATE ORDERED	DELIVERY DATE

QUOTATION NUMBER:

ITEMS	MATERIALS/Stock ORDERED FROM	ORDERED BY	DELIVERED BY

INSTRUCTIONS AS PER QUOTE: /TECHNICAL/	QUOTE TIME
INSTRUCTIONS TO PACKING	
INSTRUCTIONS (MISC.)	
PACKING AND DELIVERY TO:	

Example 9

Stock control/purchase control The areas of stock control and purchase control are obviously very closely related and can be considered together as materials management.

Questions

* Do you know the lead-time for your products?
* Are stocks kept to minimum acceptable levels for operational needs?
* Pareto's principle or the 80/20 rule can be useful in stock control; that is, does 20 per cent of your stock articles represent 80 per cent of the total stock value?
* Do you have an effective stock control system?
* Do you carry out quarterly physical stocktaking as a measure of control?
* Do you have a monthly review of stockholding?
* Do you frequently get quotes from new suppliers to check on purchasing prices?
* Can suppliers carry stock and make more frequent deliveries to you?
* Are you careful not to buy in large quantities just to obtain a discount?
* Do you have separate stock level guides for raw materials/work in progress and finished goods?
* Do you dispose of obsolete stock?
* Are you insured?

Materials management is a very important area for both manufacturing and retailing businesses; both will spend a high proportion of their anticipated sales income on the purchase of materials from outside organisations. Locking a business into one particular supplier can possibly be dangerous from the aspect of supply availability. Materials management involves not only organising sufficient materials to meet production time schedules, but also controlling the general stockholding level, since a great deal of capital can be tied up in stockholding.

It is advisable to review materials purchasing on a regular basis, to obtain quotes from alternative suppliers and also to seek discounts where available. A word of caution on discounts: it is important to evaluate 'the true cost' of carrying additional stock through bulk buyings against the benefit of a discount on a larger order.

Purchasing procedures vary enormously among different organisations, but example 9 shows one type of order form. This sort of order form contains the requisition within the job sheet itself. An alternative would be a purchase requisition, as shown in example 10.

PURCHASE REQUISITION	
Date:	Department:
Supplier nominated:	
Quantity and Description of Item(s):	
Price:	
Date Required:	
Requisitioned by:	
Authorised by:	

Example 10

The purchase requisition form is an inter-departmental form, i.e., a purchase requisition is made to the purchasing department. This procedure will initiate the ordering of materials.

Purchase analysis is obviously important as a measure of control. It can either be done at the time of placing the order, which would control the initial commitment, or at the time of receipt of the invoice. Most analysis will be done from the purchase day book; it can be carried out by account or by department.

See examples 11 and 12.

PUCHASE ANALYSIS — ACCOUNTS				
ACCOUNT		MONTH ENDED.		
DESCRIPTION	COST	OFFICE STOCK	PRODUCTION STOCK	MAINTENANCE STOCK
TOTAL				

Example 11

PUCHASE ANALYSIS BY DEPARTMENT		
	MONTH ENDED.	
ACCOUNT DESCRIPTION	COST	
	ACTUAL	BUDGET
TOTAL		

Example 12

Stock level The whole aspect of stock control is an area of conflicting interests. Businesses do not wish to run the danger of stock-outs, so the purpose of stock control is to endeavour to find a balance between the benefit of holding stocks, weighed against the disadvantage of capital tied up in stock (meaning less capital available for other purposes). Also there is the danger that stock will deteriorate or will become obsolete. In retailing, for example, the holding of 'fashionable' products may lead to quick obsolescence. Skateboards provide a good example: they were very fashionable a few years ago, but now children seem to favour roller skates once more, only this time — roller boots!

In manufacturing, of course, stockholding comprises not just basic materials but a mixture of raw materials and components, work in progress and finished goods. It is therefore important to carry out analysis of manufacturing stock. See example 13.

ANALYSIS OF MANUFACTURING STOCK MONTH ENDED.		
STOCK	£	As a %
Raw materials Work in progress Finished goods		
Total stock		

Example 13

The value of work in progress will vary enormously between different types of industrial manufacturer. Also, efficiency within the factory will affect the production cycle period, which will in turn affect the overall amount of capital tied up in work in progress as opposed to finished goods.

Stock classification A commonly used technique in stock classification is the ABC classification. This relies on the Pareto principle that a high proportion of stock value will be represented by a small number of high-cost stock items. This is also known as the 80/20 rule. Graphically this type of analysis can be shown as in Figure 2.

Figure 2 Stock control and classification

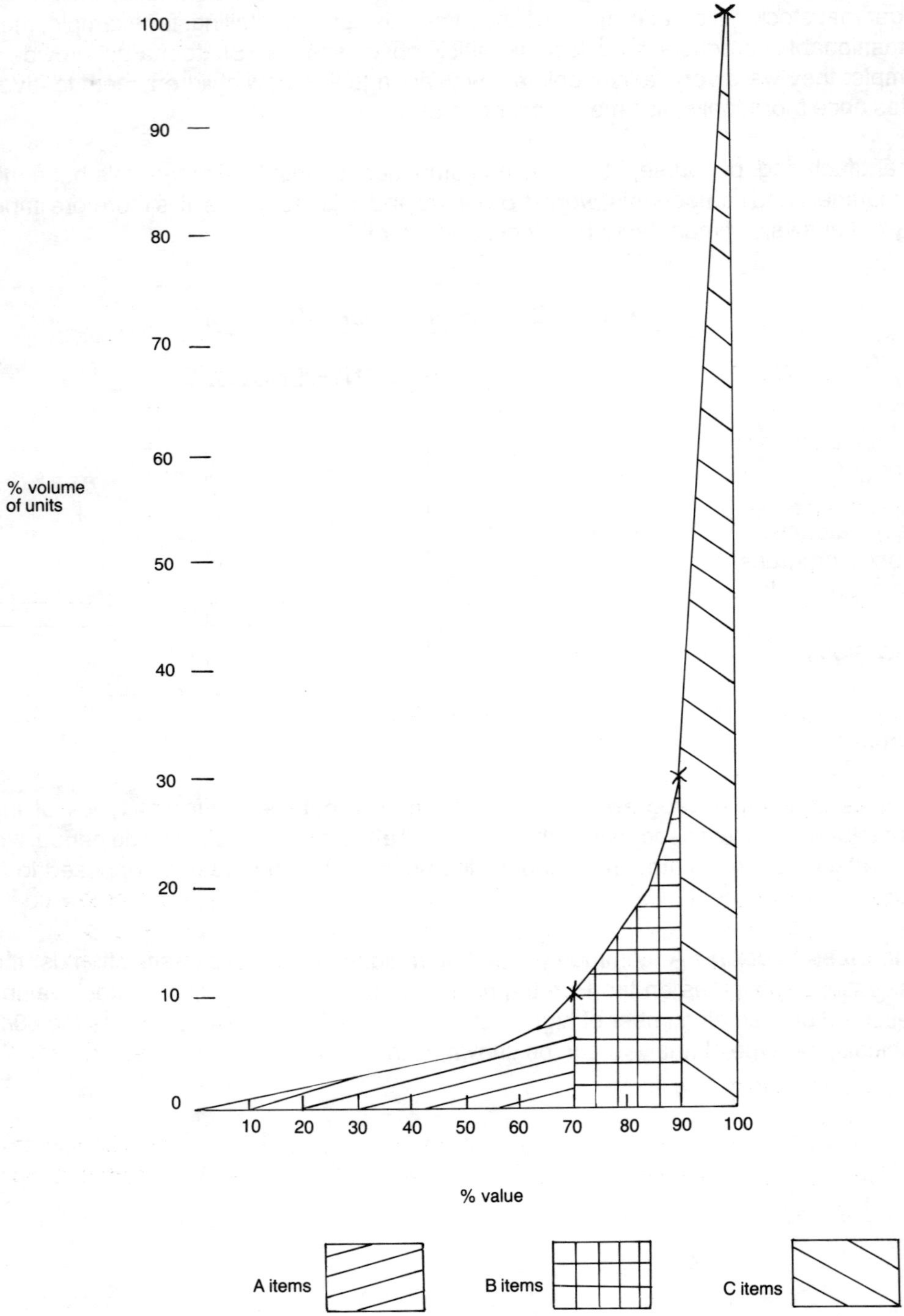

The basis of this ABC classification is that the A items, which represent 70 per cent of the total stock value in numerical terms, only represent 10 per cent of the total volume of the units held in stock. For this reason the greatest measure of control and attention can be afforded to the A items, with secondary attention being given to B items, and least to C items.

The company stock record information can be manually or computer-based, but of course whichever system is used it is important that movements are recorded accurately. A basic stock record card is illustrated in example 14.

STOCK RECORD CARD					
UNITS OR QUANTITY	DATE	REF.	STOCK IN	STOCK OUT	BALANCE
Minimum holding					
Maximum holding					
Order amount					

Example 14

Stock ordering This can be categorised into three systems:

(a) the two-bin method;
(b) the minimum stock level method;
(c) specific production method.

The two-bin method is a very simple system which is generally suitable for low-cost items — such as those referred to in our ABC analysis as 'C' items. One bin is used for materials to be issued and the other bin is held in reserve. The method is simple in that when the first bin is exhausted a requisition is made to replenish.

The minimum stock level method involves reordering when the stock record card shows the minimum holding quantity.

The third method, in ordering for specific production, is simply the requisitioning of materials requirements to fulfil works orders. With this method slow delivery from certain suppliers must be anticipated.

Stocktaking Stocktaking, particularly in manufacturing businesses, can be a very tedious and time-consuming chore. However, it is obviously very important to value the quantity of stock and materials and work in progress and on hand. Certainly for the annual audit stocks should be checked and at the same time the opportunity taken to review obsolete and redundant stocks. See example 15.

STOCK COUNT	
CATEGORY	VALUE (£)
TOTAL	

Example 15

Overheads control/analysis Business expenses may be categorised as:

(a) direct expenses, which vary with the level of production; and
(b) other expenses, which may be classified as overheads.

Basically the overhead expenses are those which do not vary in the short term with volume of turnover — for example, rent, rates, administration, salaries, etc. A good starting point is to extract from the audited accounts (in the trading and profit and loss account) those items which you could classify as business overheads, then put together an overheads budget (see Table 1).

Examples 16 and 17 show two methods of overheads analysis:

(a) by item;
(b) by department.

Overheads budget

Item	£	Actual from last account
Rent	14,500	14,000
Wages	11,000	10,050
Finance	4,000	3,620
Sundries / Depreciation	6,000	5,800
	35,500	33,470

Table 1

OVERHEADS ANALYSIS BY ITEM				
MONTH ENDED.				
ITEM	THIS MONTH		YEAR TO DATE	
	BUDGET	ACTUAL	BUDGET	ACTUAL
TOTAL				

Example 16

OVERHEADS ANALYSIS BY DEPARTMENT				
MONTH ENDED.				
DEPARTMENT	THIS MONTH		YEAR TO DATE	
	BUDGET	ACTUAL	BUDGET	ACTUAL
TOTAL				

Example 17

Now that we have seen how the objectives are translated into the technical plan, we will consider, in the next chapter, how to organise the financing of these — the financial plan.

4 The financial plan

Figure 1 shows the main elements in the financial plan.

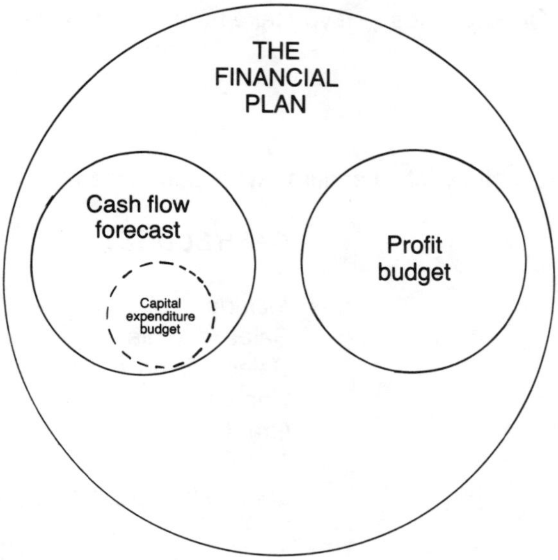

Figure 1

We will look briefly at each element before considering a simple case study to illustrate budgets in practice.

TYPES OF BUDGET

The two main budgets are:

(a) profit budget;
(b) cash flow budget (or forecast) with an associated capital expenditure budget.

It is often asked: Which comes first? The answer is that there can be little benefit in spending hours costructing a cash flow forecast if when you construct your profit budget, it projects a *loss* and not a *profit!*

Profit budget

In constructing a profit budget all we try to do is to project forward our trading and profit and loss account.

Cash flow forecast

The cash flow forecast (cash budget) is needed along with the profit budget. Most of the figures are already available in our profit budget. All we need to do is to restate the profit budget in cash terms and include any sales of fixed assets, grants receivable, or capital items purchased.

The main difference is really one of timing. For example, sales — if sold on credit there will be a delay in receipt of cash. Or purchases — if you take trade credit, payments will not be needed immediately.

Budget construction

Before going on to the case study let us confirm 'what goes where':

PROFIT BUDGET

Include
Invoiced sales
Materials *used*
All costs incurred
Interest charges only
Depreciation

Exclude
Capital expenditure
Grants
Sales of fixed assets
Loan/HP capital repayments
VAT

CASH BUDGET

Include
Sales receipts
Sales of fixed assets
Capital expenditure
Grants
Costs paid
Loans/HP repayments and interest
VAT
Creditors paid for supplies

Exclude
Depreciation

Capital expenditure budget

This may be contained within the cash flow forecast or may be presented separately, as in the following example:

CAPITAL BUDGET

	Date	Amount
Planned purchases:		£
Machinery	1.10.X3	1,500
New van	1.12.X3	2,900
Total		4,400
Less: *Disposals*		
Old van	1.12.X3	500
Net		3,900

CASE STUDY: AN INTRODUCTION TO BUDGETING

Peter Smith, aged 34, was employed as a foreman of a large company manufacturing kitchen and bedroom furniture. The company ran into difficulties and Peter Smith was made redundant.

He knew the manufacturing side of the business well and he had made similar items of furniture for friends on a private basis in his garage at home. Other orders would have been forthcoming had he been able to fulfill them. With his redundancy payment of £5,000 he decided to look into the possibility of setting up his own business. He knew there were suitable premises available in his area and that he would not have too much difficulty in finding some skilled employees.

The project

Smith decided to discuss the project in detail with a local accountant, who had been recommended to him.

Products Smith gave consideration to the product range and decided that initially he would manufacture bedside cabinets, chests of drawers and wardrobes, all these products to be in standard sizes. From experience he knew that a bedside cabinet took half an hour to produce whilst a chest of drawers took one hour and a wardrobe two hours. He knew that the material content of the units would cost approximately 40 per cent of the usual selling prices. He decided therefore that he would regard the manufacturing times for each unit as standard production times to which he could attach the wage costs of employees. Also he knew the going rate in the industry was £2.50 per hour. These facts are summarised in Table 1.

Table 1

Products	Bedside cabinets	Chests of drawers	Wardrobes
Selling price	£5	£13	£32.50
Material content per unit (40% of selling price)	£2	£5.20	£13.00
Standard production time (hours)	½	1	2
Labour cost (at £2.50 per hour)	£1.25	£2.50	£5.00

Sales forecast Again, based on experience, and after carrying-out some market research, Smith gave thought to the likely number of sales he could achieve. An agent friend confirmed that if Smith could manufacture 145 units per week he would be able to sell through established retail outlets with whom he had dealings.

The units targeted would be:

40 bedside cabinets
80 chests of drawers
25 wardrobes

145 units in total per week

This would involve production times as shown in Table 2.

Table 2

Bedside cabinets: 40 × ½ hour	=	20
Chests of drawers: 80 × 1 hour	=	80
Wardrobes: 25 × 2 hours	=	50
		150 hours

Smith knew that on the basis of a 40-hour production week per person he would need at least three employees, with himself also giving a fairly full commitment to production work.

Financial requirements As mentioned earlier, Smith had a redundancy payment of £5,000 plus his car worth £4,000. Smith thought he would require other finance, but he was not sure how much or how he would obtain it.

The accountant explained that many banks had special schemes aimed at the financing of new businesses but before lending money they liked to ensure that a project had been carefully thought out. He also told Smith that the best method of approach was to prepare a business plan, setting out in as much detail as possible the areas that had been considered and the assumptions behind the figures.

The accountant suggested the following areas for discussion.

Business plan check list

* Objectives
* Management
* Market
* Products
* Suppliers
* Physical Resources
* Personnel
* Profit and cash forecasts
* Outside finance requirement

Profitability On the basis of sales of 145 units per week the figures were extended to give weekly totals, as in Table 3.

Table 3

Sales: weekly	£	£
40 bedside cabinets at £5.00 each		200.00
80 chests of drawers at £13.00 each		1,040.00
25 wardrobes at £32.50 each		812.50
Total sales (net of VAT)		2,052.50
Less:		
Materials costs		
40 bedside cabinets at £2.00 each	80	
80 chests of drawers at £5.20 each	416	
25 wardrobes at £13.00 each	325	
	821	
Wages costs		
40 bedside cabinets at £1.25 each	50	
80 chests of drawers at £2.50 each	200	
25 wardrobes at £5.00 each	125	
	375	
Cost of sales		1,196.00
Gross profit		856.50
Gross profit (%)		41.7

This showed a gross profit of £856 per week (41.7%). The accountant explained to Smith that so far they had been looking at the variable costs in manufacturing, i.e., those costs which vary with the level of production activity. Clearly, if more production were generated then both wages and materials content would be higher, in direct proportion to the level of production.

Overheads Smith and the accountant then continued their discussion, turning to the other costs of running the business — the overheads — this time multiplying the figures out for the coming 12 months (Table 4).

Table 4 Overheads budget (12 months, net of VAT)

	£
Rent and rates	4,440
Light and heat	609
Telephone and postage	320
Administration wages and NI	2,580
Drivers' wages	4,200
Motor expenses/travelling	3,120
Insurances	1,475
Repairs and renewals	600
Accountancy/professional charges	1,200
Advertising/stationery	340
Leasing charge (machine)	1,980
Hire-purchase interest	636
Vehicle hire	3,000
Bank commission charge	200
Bank interest	931
Sundries	744
Depreciation	2,256
Proprietor withdrawals	7,500
	36,131

As shown in Table 4 the total overheads anticipated for the 12 months were £36,131.

Capital expenditure Bearing in mind that expenditure would be needed on woodworking machinery and a delivery vehicle, Smith decided to hire a vehicle on monthly contact, to save an outlay of cash.

Machinery would cost £7,000, and £5,000 of this could be purchased by hire-purchase finance; Smith would be required to find a deposit of 15 per cent of the purchase price (£750) with the capital sum and interest charges repayable over three years. The remaining £2,000 could be taken by way of a short-term leasing agreement at a cost of £165 per month.

Break-even level Smith and the accountant then calculated a projected break-even level of sales to cover materials, wages and overhead costs (Table 5).

Table 5

	£
Sales (net of VAT)	86,645
Gross profit @ 41.7%	36,131
Less: Overheads	36,131
Profit/(Loss)	Nil

The figures in Table 5 indicate a break-even level of £86,645 worth of sales required before neither profit nor loss would be encountered by the business over the next 12 months.

Profit budget Working with all the previous figures and building up sales and purchases on an annual basis, a total sales income of £98,544 was forecast, with a gross profit of £41,136 and the resulting net profit of £5,005 after a depreciation charge of £2,256 — see Table 6.

Cash flow forecast Smith felt that on average he would receive the proceeds of sale within 55 days after invoice, while he would have to pay for materials within 30 days of invoice. Having due regard for those credit timings a cash flow forecast was prepared on this basis after allowing for the introduction of Smith's capital and the payment of the deposit on the machine to be financed through hire-purchase.

The cash flow forecast showed a peak bank requirement of £10,751. This occurred in month 4 of the operating year and to allow for a little leeway the accountant suggested seeking a bank overdraft of £11,000, based on the cash flow figures shown in Table 7.

The finance was subsequently agreed by the bank manager after verification of the likely level of sales income.

Table 6 Profit budget

	Jan £	Feb £	Mar £	Apr £	May £
Sales	8,212	8,212	8,212	8,212	8,212
Forecast sales	8,212	8,212	8,212	8,212	8,212
Less:					
Materials	3,284	3,284	3,284	3,284	3,284
Manufacturing wages	1,500	1,500	1,500	1,500	1,500
Total direct costs	4,784	4,784	4,784	4,784	4,784
Gross profit	3,428	3,428	3,428	3,428	3,428
Less:					
Rent and rates	370	370	370	370	370
Light and heat	51	51	51	51	51
Telephone and postage	27	27	27	27	27
Admin. wages	215	215	215	215	215
Drivers' wages	350	350	350	350	350
Motor exp./travel	260	260	260	260	260
Insurances	123	123	123	123	123
Repairs and renewals	50	50	50	50	50
Accountancy/prof.	100	100	100	100	100
Adverts/stationery	28	28	28	28	28
Machine lease	165	165	165	165	165
HP interest	53	53	53	53	53
Vehicle hire	250	250	250	250	250
Bank charges	17	17	17	17	17
Sundries	62	62	62	62	62
Proprietor's withdrawals	625	625	625	625	625
Monthly interest	26	83	105	107	106
Trading profit	657	599	577	575	577
Less:					
Depreciation MV/Plant	188	188	188	188	188
Net profit/(loss)	469	411	389	387	389

Table 6 (cont.)

Jun £	Jul £	Aug £	Sep £	Oct £	Nov £	Dec £	Total £
8,212	8,212	8,212	8,212	8,212	8,212	8,212	98,544
8,212	8,212	8,212	8,212	8,212	8,212	8,212	98,544
3,284	3,284	3,284	3,284	3,284	3,284	3,284	39,408
1,500	1,500	1,500	1,500	1,500	1,500	1,500	18,000
4,784	4,784	4,784	4,784	4,784	4,784	4,784	57,408
3,428	3,428	3,428	3,428	3,428	3,428	3,428	41,136
370	370	370	370	370	370	370	4,440
51	51	51	51	51	51	51	609
27	27	27	27	27	27	27	320
215	215	215	215	215	215	215	2,580
350	350	350	350	350	350	350	4,200
260	260	260	260	260	260	260	3,120
123	123	123	123	123	123	123	1,475
50	50	50	50	50	50	50	600
100	100	100	100	100	100	100	1,200
28	28	28	28	28	28	28	340
165	165	165	165	165	165	165	1,980
53	53	53	53	53	53	53	636
250	250	250	250	250	250	250	3,000
17	17	17	17	17	17	17	200
62	62	62	62	62	62	62	744
625	625	625	625	625	625	625	7,500
85	88	86	65	68	66	46	931
598	595	597	617	615	617	637	7,261
188	188	188	188	188	188	188	2,256
410	407	409	429	427	429	449	5,005

Table 7 Cash flow forecast

	Jan £	Feb £	Mar £	Apr £	May £
Sales receipts	0	1,574	9,444	9,444	9,444
Capital introduced	5,000	0	0	0	0
Total receipts	5,000	1,574	9,444	9,444	9,444
Less:					
Materials	3,284	3,284	3,284	3,284	3,284
Manufacturing wages	1,500	1,500	1,500	1,500	1,500
Rent and rates	370	370	370	370	370
Light and heat	0	0	155	0	0
Telephone and postage	5	5	70	5	5
Admin. wages	215	215	215	215	215
Drivers' wages	350	350	350	350	350
Motor exp./travel	260	260	260	260	260
Insurances	1,475	0	0	0	0
Repairs and renewals	50	50	50	50	50
Accountancy/prof.	100	100	100	100	100
Adverts/stationery	120	20	20	20	20
Machine lease	165	165	165	165	165
HP interest	53	53	53	53	53
Vehicle hire	250	250	250	250	250
Bank charges	0	0	50	0	0
Sundries	62	62	62	62	62
Proprietor's withdrawals	625	625	625	625	625
Overdraft interest	0	0	214	0	0
Machine deposit	750	0	0	0	0
VAT	0	0	0	3,695	0
HP capital	118	118	118	118	118
Total payments	9,752	7,427	7,911	11,122	7,427
Net cash flow	−4,752	−5,853	1,533	−1,678	2,017
Opening bank balance	0	−4,752	−10,605	−9,073	−10,751
Closing bank balance	−4,752	−10,605	−9,073	−10,751	−8,734

*Minor discrepancies in totals are due to rounding up or down of figures on computer.

Table 7 (cont.)

Jun £	Jul £	Aug £	Sep £	Oct £	Nov £	Dec £	Total £
9,444	9,444	9,444	9,444	9,444	9,444	9,444	96,012
0	0	0	0	0	0	0	5,000
9,444	9,444	9,444	9,444	9,444	9,444	9,444	101,012
3,284	3,284	3,284	3,284	3,284	3,284	3,284	39,408
1,500	1,500	1,500	1,500	1,500	1,500	1,500	18,000
370	370	370	370	370	370	370	4,440
129	0	0	150	0	0	175	609
70	5	5	70	5	5	70	320
215	215	215	215	215	215	215	2,580
350	350	350	350	350	350	350	4,200
260	260	260	260	260	260	260	3,120
0	0	0	0	0	0	0	1,475
50	50	50	50	50	50	50	600
100	100	100	100	100	100	100	1,200
20	20	20	20	20	20	20	340
165	165	165	165	165	165	165	1,980
53	53	53	53	53	53	53	636
250	250	250	250	250	250	250	3,000
50	0	0	50	0	0	50	200
62	62	62	62	62	62	62	744
625	625	625	625	625	625	625	7,500
298	0	0	239	0	0	179	931
0	0	0	0	0	0	0	750
0	3,695	0	0	3,695	0	0	11,086
118	118	118	118	118	118	118	1,416
7,969	11,122	7,427	7,931	11,122	7,427	7,896	104,535
1,475	−1,679	2,017	1,533	−1,679	2,017	1,548	−3,523 *
−8,734	−7,260	−8,938	−6,921	−5,409	−7,089	−5,070	
−7,260	−8,938	−6,921	−5,409	−7,087	−5,070	−3,523 *	

5 The importance of monitoring business performance

This is a key area. In today's competitive business environment it is not sufficient to set objectives, draw up budgets and then ignore actual progress against these targets. The monitoring of business performance is *vital* in that it can quickly alert both banker and customer to possible problems. The following case study illustrates this point.

CASE STUDY: HEEDING THE WARNING SIGNALS

Background

For many years David Allen ran a successful business as a retailer of high-class glass and chinaware. He operated four shops in the south-east of England, three of which were in small towns and one on the coast at a busy summer holiday centre.

Each shop was run by an individual manager with Mr Allen directing overall operations. All the businesses were in rented premises. Early in 19X7 Mr Allen suffered a stroke and retired from the business.

Control of the business then passed to his son Charles, who had recently completed a business studies course at a local college. Charles knew that his father had not had any formal management or financial training and had basically run the business using his experience in the trade and what he described as a feeling for the way things were going.

He knew that his father had not been too pleased in recent months with the way things were going at the shops and that he had had several meetings with the bank manager concerning the overdraft facility. Charles decided to make a full review as though he were purchasing the business.

Financial accounts

The financial accounts for the previous three years were as follows.

Trading results

Year ended	*31.1.X4*	*31.1.X5*	*31.1.X6*
Sales	£185,321	£200,471	£225,458
Gross profit	£89,139	£94,822	£104,887
Gross profit %	48.1	47.3	46.5
Overheads	£81,100	£88,522	£102,207
% of sales	43.7	44.1	45.3
Net profit/(loss)	8,039	6,300	2,680

The balance sheet as at 31.1.X6 showed the following position.

Balance sheet as at 31.1.X6

Liabilities:	£	Assets:	£
Creditors	16,977	Stock	97,990
Bank	21,968	Debtors	4,940
		Cash in hand	376
Current liabilities	38,945	Current assets	103,306
Issued capital	25,000		
Profit and loss account balance	60,668	Fixed assets	14,907
		Goodwill	6,400
	124,613		124,613

Interpretation The trading results for the three years to January 19X6 looked satisfactory at first glance. However, on closer examination:

(a) Sales had hardly kept pace with inflation running through that period and had shown little real growth.

(b) Profit margins were slowly falling away, as was shown when the gross profit percentages were compared.

(c) Overheads were increasing.

(d) Profitability was falling away and it was over a year since the last figures were extracted.

(e) The balance sheet, however, looked fairly strong with a good measure of liquidity (that is, the amount the current assets exceed the current liabilities). Also there was a sound 'net worth' base (that is, total assets less liabilities).

Due to the historic nature of the figures it was therefore imperative for Charles to know the up-to-date situation and he called in the company's accountant to audit the books for the year to 31 January 19X7. Meanwhile, several creditors were pressing for payment and it was necessary to renegotiate an overdraft facility of £62,000 at the bank, based on the long-established track record of the business, in order to keep the creditors happy.

Current situation

In July 19X7 Charles received the following summary of trading for the year ended 31 January 19X7.

Trading and profit and loss account for the 12-month period ending on 31.1.X7

Sales	£228,578
Gross profit	£96,688
Gross profit %	42.3
Less:	
Overheads	£124,242
% of sales	54.3
Loss on trading	(£27,554)

Summarised balance sheet as at 31.1.X7

Liabilities:	£	£	Assets:	£
Creditors		48,191	Stock	119,144
Bank		44,000	Debtors	8,495
			Cash in hand	566
Current liabilities		92,191	Current assets	128,205
Issued capital		25,000	Fixed assets	15,700
Profit and loss account:			Goodwill	6,400
Brought forward:	60,668			
Less: Loss	27,554			
	33,114	33,114		
		150,305		150,305

Interpretation The trading account revealed a large loss of £27,554. Bearing in mind these figures were for the period to the end of January 19X7, they were already out of date. It was more than likely that further monies had been lost in the first six months of trading in 19X7. Charles was therefore very worried about the position and asked the accountant to prepare figures to bring him right up to date, i.e., from the 1 January 19X7 to 30 June 19X7. Looking at the figures in the balance sheet as at 31.1.X7, stock had increased together with a rising bank overdraft and creditor position, compared with the previous year. Sales as shown in the trading and profit and loss account to 31.1.X7 had increased only marginally to £228,000, which together with a reduced gross profit percentage and rising overhead costs meant a loss in trading in the year of £27,554.

Charles was of course worried as any further losses would further deteriorate the net worth of the business. So pending management action Charles decided to visit immediately each shop in turn with the following points in mind:

(a) Premises — site and tenure, location, suitability for future development.

(b) Management — experience, age and responsibility, general staffing.

(c) Market — what was the local competition and could the firm compare both on price and quality?

(d) Products — were they satisfying customers' needs?

(e) Costing and pricing — how were the prices of the products arrived at? Did each manager keep individual records of costs in the shops?

(f) Stock control — was it adequate?

(g) Trading performance — sales, cost of sales, overheads, profitability?

Interim accounts

The accountant produced interim accounts for the first six months of 19X7 which showed the following position.

Trading and profit and loss account: 1.1.X7 to 3.5.X7

Sales	£108,350
Gross profit	£46,870
Gross profit %	43
Less:	
Overheads	65,010
% of sales	60
Loss on trading	(£18,140)

Balance sheet as at 30.6.X7

Liabilities:	£	£	Assets:	£
Creditors		66,837	Stock	124,310
Bank		45,070	Debtors	6,421
Current liabilities		111,907	Current assets	130,731
Issued capital		25,000	Fixed assets	14,750
Profit and loss account:			Goodwill	6,400
Brought forward	33,114			
Less: Loss	18,140			
		14,974		
		151,881		151,881

Corrective action

Armed with these more up-to-date figures, Charles immediately called a meeting of all the shop managers, at which his accountant agreed to be present to explain the results of the first six months of 19X7.

The shop managers were obviously concerned at the changing pattern of results from those that had been experienced over previous years. They gave Charles an explanation that demand had fallen away from the company's traditionally high class merchandise and it was decided at the meeting to extend the range of merchandise to include some cheaper product lines. Also in view of the high stock position at many of the shops, sales were to be held with the aim of generating cash to allow Charles to pay pressing creditors and to reduce the amount of borrowed money in the business.

Charles reviewed the net worth of the shops with his accountant and it was decided:

(a) The development of a new town shopping centre precinct had deprived one shop of a substantial catchment area, but since the shop manager still saw potential in the site a deal was agreed whereby he could purchase the business from Charles.

(b) An outlying shop in a market town was making little contribution to sales and plans were made to sell off the business on the manager's imminent retirement.

Charles felt that the two remaining shops were well sited and had good, enthusiastic managers., Based on this rationalisation scheme, in conjunction with his accountant, Charles prepared a profit budget and cash budget for the coming year. He carefully made a note of the assumptions on which his budgets were to be based. He began by preparing a sales budget for both shops in conjunction with the shop managers. Sales were estimated to total £63,500 for shop A and £69,000 for shop B, giving total sales of £132,500.

Sales budget: July 19X7 to June 19X8

	Jul	Aug	Sep	Oct	Nov	Dec	Jan	Feb	Mar	Apr	May	Jun	Total
	£	£	£	£	£	£	£	£	£	£	£	£	
Town shop A	5,700	4,500	4,750	5,000	4,000	11,000	3,300	3,750	4,600	6,700	5,000	5,200	63,500
Coast shop B	10,000	8,500	7,000	3,000	3,000	6,000	3,000	3,500	4,500	5,000	7,000	8,500	69,000
	15,700	13,000	11,750	8,000	7,000	17,000	6,300	7,250	9,100	11,700	12,000	13,700	132,500

He then prepared the associated overheads budget for each shop, plus an overheads charge for the administration of the business.

Overheads budget: July 19X7 to June 19X8 (net of VAT)

	Town shop A	Coast shop B	Administration	Total
Wages and NI	8,152	10,100		18,252
Casual wages	2,000	4,000	—	6,000
Rent and rates	3,500	4,100	—	7,600
Heat and light	750	850	—	1,600
Insurances	—	—	1,250	1,250
Motor expenses	—	—	2,448	2,448
Telephone charges	170	180	—	350
Repairs and renewals	500	496	—	996
Printing, stationery, adverts and postage	250	250	100	600
Bank charges and interest	—	—	4,315	4,315
Audit and accountancy	—	—	1,250	1,250
Hire-purchase interest	—	—	—	—
Professional charges	—	—	100	100
Sundry expenses	150	150	—	300
Depreciation, motor vehicles and equipment	250	250	2,500	3,000
Directors' remuneration	—	—	5,004	5,004
Totals	15,722	20,376	16,967	53,065

Using the data base of the sales forecast, purchases were forecast to meet these sales needs and then the figures were all amalgamated in profit budget for the restructured business.

Profit budget July 19X7 to June 19X8 (after rationalisation scheme)

	Jul	Aug	Sep	Oct	Nov	Dec
	£	£	£	£	£	£
Shop sales	15,700	13,000	11,750	8,000	7,000	17,000
Forecast sales	15,700	13,000	11,750	8,000	7,000	17,000
Less:						
Forecast purchases	8,949	7,410	6,698	4,560	3,990	9,690
Total direct costs	8,949	7,410	6,698	4,560	3,990	9,690
Gross profit	6,751	5,590	5,053	3,440	3,010	7,310
Less:						
Wages and NI	1,521	1,521	1,521	1,521	1,521	1,521
Casual wages	500	500	500	500	500	500
Rent and rates	633	633	633	633	633	633
Heat and light	133	133	133	133	133	133
Insurances	104	104	104	104	104	104
Motor expenses	204	204	204	204	204	204
Telephone	29	29	29	29	29	29
Repairs and renewals	83	83	83	83	83	83
Stationery/advertising	50	50	50	50	50	50
Bank charges	0	0	50	0	0	50
Audit and accountancy	104	104	104	104	104	104
Professional charges	8	8	8	8	8	8
Sundries	25	25	25	25	25	25
Directors' remuneration	417	417	417	417	417	417
Monthly interest	332	366	329	344	353	347
Trading profit/(loss)	2,607	1,411	861	(716)	(1,156)	3,101
Less:						
Depreciation	250	250	250	250	250	250
Net profit/(loss)	2,357	1,161	611	(966)	(1,406)	2,851

Profit budget (cont.)

Jan	Feb	Mar	Apr	May	Jun	Total
£	£	£	£	£	£	£
6,300	7,250	9,100	11,700	12,000	13,700	132,500
6,300	7,250	9,100	11,700	12,000	13,700	132,500
3,591	4,133	5,187	6,669	6,840	7,809	75,525
3,591	4,133	5,187	6,669	6,840	7,809	75,525
2,709	3,118	3,913	5,031	5,160	5,891	56,975
1,521	1,521	1,521	1,521	1,521	1,521	18,252
500	500	500	500	500	500	6,000
633	633	633	633	633	633	7,600
133	133	133	133	133	133	1,600
104	104	104	104	104	104	1,250
204	204	204	204	204	204	2,448
29	29	29	29	29	29	350
83	83	83	83	83	83	996
50	50	50	50	50	50	600
0	0	50	0	0	50	200
104	104	104	104	104	104	1,250
8	8	8	8	8	8	100
25	25	25	25	25	25	300
417	417	417	417	417	417	5,004
349	339	336	355	349	318	4,115
(1,452)	(1,034)	(286)	863	999	1,711	6,910
250	250	250	250	250	250	3,000
(1,702)	(1,284)	(536)	613	749	1,461	3,910

Cash budget July 19X7 to June 19X8 (after rationalisation scheme)

	Jul £	Aug £	Sep £	Oct £	Nov £	Dec £
Sales receipts	6,000	18,055	14,950	13,513	9,200	8,050
Total receipts	6,000	18,055	14,950	13,513	9,200	8,050
Purchase payments	10,025	10,291	8,522	7,702	5,244	4,589
Wages and NI	1,521	1,521	1,521	1,521	1,521	1,521
Casual wages	500	500	500	500	500	500
Rent and rates	1,900	0	0	1,900	0	0
Heat and light	0	0	300	0	0	500
Insurances	0	0	1,250	0	0	0
Motor expenses	204	204	204	204	204	204
Telephone	0	85	0	0	85	0
Repairs and renewals	83	83	83	83	83	83
Stationery/advertising	50	50	50	50	50	50
Bank charges	0	0	50	0	0	50
Audit and accountancy	0	0	0	1,250	0	0
Professional charges	0	0	0	50	0	0
Sundries	25	25	25	25	25	25
Directors' remuneration	417	417	417	417	417	417
Overdraft interest	0	0	1,026	0	0	1,044
VAT	2,500	0	0	2,069	0	0
Total payments	17,225	13,176	13,948	16,311	8,129	8,982
Net cash flow	−11,225	4,879	1,002	−2,799	1,071	−932
Opening bank balance	−25,000	−36,225	−31,346	−30,344	−33,143	−32,072
Closing bank balance	−36,225	−31,346	−30,344	−33,143	−32,072	−33,004
	peak balance					

Cash budget (cont.)

Jan	Feb	Mar	Apr	May	Jun	Total
£	£	£	£	£	£	£
19,550	7,245	8,338	10,465	13,455	13,800	142,620
19,550	7,245	8,338	10,465	13,455	13,800	142,620
11,144	4,103	4,752	5,965	7,669	7,866	87,898
1,521	1,521	1,521	1,521	1,521	1,521	18,252
500	500	500	500	500	500	6,000
1,900	0	0	1,900	0	0	7,600
0	0	500	0	0	300	1,600
0	0	0	0	0	0	1,250
204	204	204	204	204	204	2,448
0	90	0	0	90	0	350
83	83	83	83	83	83	996
50	50	50	50	50	50	600
0	0	50	0	0	50	200
0	0	0	0	0	0	1,250
0	0	0	50	0	0	100
25	25	25	25	25	25	300
417	417	417	417	417	417	5,004
0	0	1,023	0	0	1,022	4,115
2,064	0	0	1,461	0	0	8,634
17,908	7,020	9,126	12,176	10,559	12,038	146,598
1,642	225	−788	−1,711	2,896	1,762	−3,978
−33,004	−31,362	−31,136	−31,924	−33,635	−30,740	
−31,362	−31,137	−31,924	−33,635	−30,739	−28,978	

On examination of the figures in the profit budget a forecast annual profit of £3,910 was disclosed. Using this profit budget as a base and having due regard for the timing of payments and purchases a cash budget was produced for the same period and this indicated a peak bank borrowing requirement of £36,225 (for the rationalised business).

This peak bank facility was agreed by the bank manager on the basis that the disposal of the two shops would reduce the bank balance to that shown within the cash flow, i.e., an opening balance of £25,000 in July.

Conclusion

The hiving down or rationalisation of any business is always a difficult step to take. Charles saw this action as the only way out of his dilemma. There may have been other ways, such as an injection of new monies into the business from an outside investor; however, he did manage to return the business, albeit in a restructured form, to profitable trading.

This case study clearly illustrates the need to keep up to date as much as possible in monitoring the financial progress of any business. If the problems had been seen earlier perhaps there would have been no need to dispose of the two shops.

SUMMARY

Bankers do not need to be expert at production of any of the budgets we have studied. However, a working knowledge of these documents is necessary in order to be able to deal with the crux of the matter from the banker's point of view — assessing the lending proposition.

Part Two

Assessing the business lending proposition

6 The key areas

The key areas which need to be examined are:

(a) the customer and his business;
(b) asset cover for the advance (and security);
(c) repayment ability/serviceability of debt;
(d) monitoring of performance.

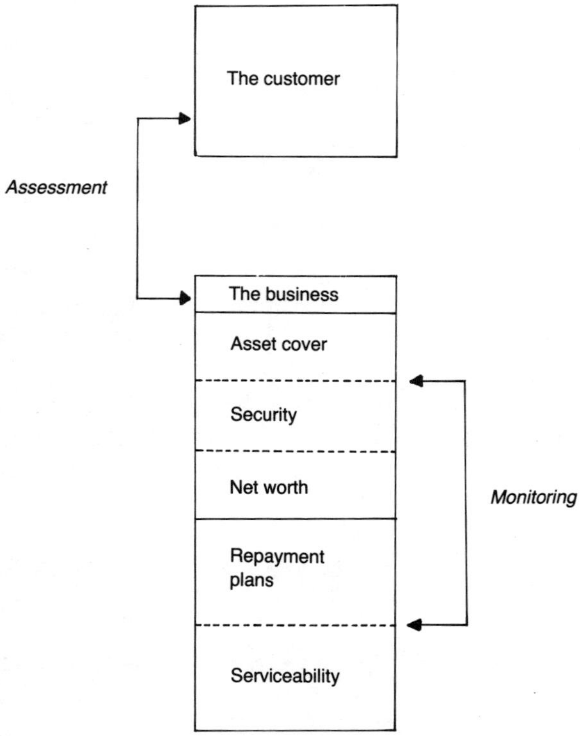

Figure 1 Key areas of assessment

These areas are shown diagrammatically in Figure 1. This diagram should be studied carefully in order to avoid the pitfalls of lending to the applicant with little regard to the business, its net worth or serviceability; or lending to the applicant plus securing the debt, but with little regard to serviceability! If any of the key areas is ignored, problems will be encountered sooner or later. A full assessment must be made to reach a balanced judgment.

It is vitally important to remember that a business, no matter how strong its balance sheet, cannot carry a debt burden greater than can be serviced by the income earning capacity of the business. It is for this reason that great emphasis will be placed on understanding the *trading* 'profile' of the business. This is displayed in the trading and profit and loss account and is projected in the profit budget.

In the remainder of this chapter we will consider how to assess the customer, and in subsequent chapters how to assess the business. As with other lending, there is no mathematical formula to make life very easy (and probably boring)! Every business is different in structure, size, layout and facilities. The financial resources of the business will also vary. It is a different proposition to lend £20,000 to a business with total assets of, say, £100,000, than to lend the same amount to one with total assets of £20,000. Also, if you lend £20,000 for working capital, then the cash return to the business will be different from £20,000 lent to buy a new machine which may only 'return' less costs in fuel, repairs, etc.

ESSENTIAL REQUIREMENTS

The five basic points to consider for any type of bank lending are:

(a) How much is required?
(b) What is to be done with the money?
(c) What are the plans for repayment?
(d) What will be the bank's position if the plans for repayment go wrong?
(e) What is the experience and track record of the borrower?

If you look again at Chapter 4, The Financial Plan, then it should be possible to answer many of these questions from the documents essential in financial planning. If these are all not available then the customer, or his adviser, should be asked to complete them. The following are essential:

(a) *The cash flow forecast* will tell us what is to be done with the money and how much is required.

(b) The plans for repayment will be illustrated in the *cash flow forecast* and the feasibility of any repayments will be shown by looking at any margin available in the *profit budget* together with the record of past profits in the *audited accounts.*

(c) If things go wrong, then the 'buffer' or net worth is illustrated in the past *audited accounts.*

VISITING THE BUSINESS

This is also essential and will yield a lot of information. Most people are very receptive and only too willing to show you around.

Observation and discussion will enable you to make a judgement as to technical and management ability.

* What is the customer's experience?
* How long has he been in business?
* Does he use modern techniques?
* Is he in full control or does he spend a lot of time away?
* What is his depth of management ability and who is there to help him?
* Does he delegate routine tasks?
* Who keeps the business records?

Also you will see the business size and learn about the products, the state of buildings and machinery. Does the place look well organised? Have the buildings and machinery the capacity to meet production plans? Look at the plans and discuss them.

All this information will help you when going on to contemplate the *financial picture* of the business. A check list for recording a visit is given at the end of this chapter.

TECHNICAL ABILITY OF THE CUSTOMER

A key feature in the analysis of any lending proposition is the technical ability of the customer — can he perform the tasks required of him to make enough money for successful repayment? Can mechanics repair cars effectively, can plumbers install central heating appliances without leaving leaks, can builders lay bricks to the standards required by the surveyors from the local authority or the building society? There will be no profit or source of repayment if the applicant does not have the skills to satisfy reasonable customers — they will simply refuse to pay.

CASE STUDY: THE CUSTOMER'S EXPERTISE

A builder asks for an advance of £10,000. He does not have an account with the bank but he has bought a small terraced property from his redundancy payment, cost £4,000. The property has been occupied by an old lady and needs substantial renovations and he expects that these will cost £10,000 including parts and labour. He will be able to sell the refurbished property for £22,000 — an estate agent's letter is available confirming that a ready market is available for this type of property. The refurbishment will take three months to complete.

Summary

	£		£
Cost	4,000	Expected sale price	22,000
Refurbishment	10,000	Less: Legal fees and expenses	1,000
	14,000		
Expected surplus	7,000		
	21,000		21,000

Security Offered first mortgage over the property, ultimate value to be £22,000.

Since this is a self-liquidating deal with an adequate margin of £7,000 in the sale price with full security cover, the bank manager agrees the advance of £10,000 on overdraft — monies to be drawn as required.

The month end figures from the bank account reveal the following:

Month	Best	Worst	Limit
	£	£	£
1	1,000 Dr	2,500 Dr	10,000 Dr
2	2,500 Dr	5,300 Dr	10,000 Dr
3	5,300 Dr	7,800 Dr	10,000 Dr
4	7,800 Dr	10,300 Dr	10,000 Dr

At this stage the project is now one month overdue but comforted by the adequate margins and the security the manager does nothing.

In month 5 the worst balance reaches 12,500 Dr, at which stage the manager calls for a report from the customer and is disappointed to discover that there have been 'some problems' which have now been resolved but 'there is still a little more work to do — another £1,000 should be sufficient'.

In month 6 the worst balance reaches £14,500 Dr but the job is now complete and a sale has been arranged. Unfortunately when the building society's surveyor inspects the property he discovers that the standard of work is *appalling*! He values the property at £18,000 maximum and he is not prepared to recommend the advance unless further work, estimated at £5,000, is undertaken by a qualified craftsman.

Summary after six months

	£
Total cost + refurbishments	18,500
Expected cost of alterations	5,000
	23,500
Add: Legal costs	1,000
	24,500
Expected sale price	18,000
Shortfall	6,500

The bank is now faced with a potential bad debt caused by the customer's inability to carry out the building work to a satisfactory standard.

Conclusion

Whilst many propositions may appear to be self-liquidating it is vital to ensure that the customer has the ability technically to fulfil his side of the deal. This aspect does cause the banker problems but he does have some guidelines which can help in his assessment:

* Does the customer have trade qualifications?
  Track record evidenced by retained profits in the balance sheet?

* Local reputation?
  Extra care should always be taken with customers who have just set up in business or who are unable to show evidence of a track record.

BUSINESS VISIT CHECK LIST

The following notes may be useful when carrying out a business visit:

Date:

Business name and address:

Buildings:
owned/tenanted: Rent:
machinery:

Management structure

Products: Price:

Labour availability:

Financial data: available: √ not available: X
(i) Balance sheet and accounts
(ii) Product information
(iii) Profit budget
(iv) Management accounts
(v) Cash planning
(vi) Corporate plan

Existing level of funding:
(i) Overdraft: £
(ii) Loan: £
(iii) Other finance: £

Proposed funding:
(Working capital/Fixed asset purchase)
(i) Overdraft: £
(ii) Loan: £
(iii) Other: £

Gearing:
(i) Capital
(ii) Interest cover

The key areas

Serviceability/Cash flow:
Check: satisfactory √   unsatisfactory: X

(i) Profit budget
(ii) Cash flow
(iii) Audited accounts
(iv) Bank statistic trends

Security:

Summary:

Comment on:

(i) Management ability
(ii) Track record
(iii) Level of finance requested
(iv) Repayment ability
(v) Security offered

---

7 Financial performance

BANK RECORDS

This is where the banker is fortunate. He has all the usual bank records available to him. Examination of the bank statements will reveal:

* Business turnover
* Average bank balance
* Range of the account
* Standing orders and direct debits and any unpaid cheques

Comparison of these statistics with previous years will help paint the financial picture, e.g., falling turnover coupled with an increasing debit balance will merit close investigation!

AUDITED ACCOUNTS

The accounts could well be historic but it is well worth looking at them. Most banks have forms for extracting ratios. What we are looking for is a *'reasonable'* balance between net worth and debt. Other ratios will give us indications of liquidity, debt serviceability and trading performance.

There are numerous ratios that can be used, but it is sufficient for our purposes to consider only the main ones. The following case study will take us into ratio analysis.

CASE STUDY: USING RATIOS

The banking facilities available from XYZ Bank for two companies as at the end of 19X6 were as follows:

Light Engineering Ltd:

	£		£
O/D	60,000	Security:	
Loan	18,000	1st charge company premises:	
	———	Freehold value	55,000
	78,000	Debenture	
	———		

Clothing Imports Ltd:

	£		£
Overdraft and/or irrevocable		Security:	
documentary credits	200,000	1st charge company premises:	
	———	Freehold value	60,000
	200,000	Debenture	
	———		

The following comprise extracts from the financial accounts of these two typical, private limited company customers. As the names suggest, Light Engineering Ltd is engaged in the manufacture of light machinery mainly against firm orders. Clothing Imports Ltd is a merchant engaged in the import and subsequent wholesale of ready made-up fashion clothing from the Far East.

Profit and loss accounts

	Light Engineering Ltd						Clothing Imports Ltd		
		19X4		19X5		19X6	19X4	19X5	19X6
	£	£	£	£	£	£	£	£	£
Sales		200,000		220,000		210,000	900,000	1,050,000	1,300,000
Materials consumed	55,000		66,000		59,000		810,000	956,000	1,209,000
Direct labour	75,000		81,000		80,000		—	—	—
Cost of goods sold		130,000		147,000		139,000	810,000	956,000	1,209,000
Gross profit		70,000		73,000		71,000	90,000	94,000	91,000
Admin. and distribution expenses		59,000		60,500		59,500	57,000	59,500	78,000
Operating profit		11,000		12,500		11,500	33,000	34,500	13,000
Interest paid		5,000		5,500		6,500	8,000	8,500	11,00
Profit before tax		6,000		7,000		5,000	25,000	26,000	2,000
Tax		2,000		2,200		1,000	8,000	10,000	—
Attributable profit after tax		4,000		4,800		4,000	17,000	16,000	2,000

Balance sheets

	Light Engineering Ltd			Clothing Imports Ltd		
	19X4	19X5	19X6	19X4	19X5	19X6
Current assets:	£	£	£	£	£	£
Cash	1,000	1,000	—	—	—	—
Debtors	44,000	51,000	46,000	150,000	170,000	230,000
Quick assets	45,000	52,000	46,000	150,000	170,000	230,000
Stock	10,000	15,000	15,000	135,000	190,000	257,000
Work in progress	25,000	29,000	25,000	—	—	—
Total current assets	80,000	96,000	86,000	285,000	360,000	487,000
Current liabilities:						
Creditors	9,000	13,000	11,000	140,000	180,000	280,000
Hire-purchase	1,000	1,000	1,000	2,000	2,000	2,000
Bank	38,000	47,000	43,000	90,000	105,000	138,000
Tax	1,500	1,700	500	8,000	10,000	5,000
Directors' loans	4,500	6,500	5,000	10,000	10,000	10,000
Total current liabilities	54,000	69,200	60,500	250,000	307,000	435,000
Net current assets	26,000	26,800	25,500	35,000	53,000	52,000
Fixed assets:						
Property at cost	35,000	35,000	35,000	36,000	36,000	36,000
Net current value	(45,000)	(50,000)	(55,000)	(60,000)	(60,000)	(60,000)
Machinery and plant	47,000	45,000	55,000	5,000	4,000	3,000
Fixtures and fittings	2,500	3,000	2,200	2,000	2,000	4,000
Motor vehicles	8,000	7,000	5,000	8,000	6,000	10,000
Total fixed assets	92,500	90,000	97,200	51,000	48,000	53,000
Deferred liability:						
Bank loans	20,000	19,000	18,000	—	—	—
Long-term HP	13,500	8,000	10,900	6,000	5,000	7,000
Total deferred liability	33,500	27,000	28,900	6,000	5,000	7,000
Net tangible assets	85,000	89,800	93,800	80,000	96,000	98,000
Share capital	40,000	40,000	40,000	20,000	20,000	20,000
P & L account	45,000	49,800	53,800	60,000	76,000	78,000
Shareholders' funds	85,000	89,800	93,800	80,000	96,000	98,000

Source and application of funds statements

		Light Engineering Ltd			Clothing Imports Ltd	
		19X5	19X6		19X5	19X6
Source of funds:		£	£		£	£
Profit before tax		7,000	5,000		26,000	2,000
Depreciation		8,200	10,000		2,000	2,000
Funds generated by operations	(A)	15,200	15,000		28,000	4,000
Application of funds:						
Purchase of fixed assets		5,700	17,200	(Sale)	(1,000)	7,000
Tax paid		2,000	2,200		8,000	5,000
	(B)	7,700	19,400		7,000	12,000
Net funds generated (absorbed) (A-B)	(C)	7,500	(4,400)		21,000	(8,000)
Working capital change*	(D)	(10,000)	5,500		(35,000)	(27,000)
Funds available for repayment of bank & HP liabilities (C-D)		(2,500)	1,100		(14,000)	(35,000)
Increase (decrease) in long-term debt		(6,500)	1,900		(1,000)	2,000
Increase (decrease) in net short-term debt		9,000	(3,000)		15,000	33,000
		2,500	(1,100)		14,000	35,000

*Working capital change:

	Light Engineering Ltd 19X5	Light Engineering Ltd 19X6	Clothing Imports Ltd 19X5	Clothing Imports Ltd 19X6
Increase (decrease) in creditors	6,000	(3,500)	40,000	100,000
Less: Increase (decrease) in debtors	7,000	(5,000)	20,000	60,000
Less: Increase (decrease) in stock	9,000	(4,000)	55,000	67,000
	(10,000)	5,500	(35,000)	(27,000)

The extracts are not from complex financial accounts, but they do contain a good deal of information. Three years' figures are shown, in order to form an assessment of the quality of the customer's business performance and underlying strength. Three years is considered the minimum from which to glean meaningful trends.

CAPITAL GEARING

The most common ratio extracted by bankers is the capital gearing ratio. To simplify comparison of trends we will calculate this as a percentage. It is defined as:

$$\frac{\text{Actual borrowed money}}{\text{Net worth}} = \frac{\text{Actual usage of lines of credit}}{\text{Shareholders' funds}} \times 100$$

i.e., *borrowed money expressed as a % of net worth*

	19X4	19X5	19X6
Light Engineering Ltd:	£	£	£
Actual borrowed money:			
Bank O/D	38,000	47,000	43,000
Bank loan	20,000	19,000	18,000
Current and deferred HP	14,500	9,000	11,900
Directors' loans	4,500	6,500	5,000
	77,000	81,500	77,900
Net worth	85,000	89,800	93,800
Capital gearing ratio	91%	91%	83%
Clothing Imports Ltd:			
Actual borrowed money:			
Bank O/D	90,000	105,000	138,000
Current and deferred HP	8,000	7,000	9,000
Directors' loans	10,000	10,000	10,000
	108,000	122,000	157,000
Net worth	80,000	96,000	98,000
Capital gearing ratio	135%	127%	160%

Having arrived at these capital gearing ratios it is now necessary to *qualify* our calculations.

(a) Capital gearing adjusted for directors' loans

The above calculations include directors' loans as actual borrowed money — in the numerator of the ratio. Such loans may or may not be interest-bearing. If they are not interest-bearing, it could be argued that they are a form of shareholders' funds, in which case they could be subtracted from the borrowed money side of the ratio, and added on to the shareholders' funds or net worth side of the ratio. If we amend the ratios for the two companies to reflect this, the situation will be as follows:

	19X4	19X5	19X6
Light Engineering Ltd:	£	£	£
Actual borrowed money (as above)	77,000	81,500	77,900
Less: Directors' loans	4,500	6,500	5,000
Revised actual borrowed money	72,500	75,000	72,900
Net worth (as above)	85,000	89,800	93,800
Add: Directors' loans	4,500	6,500	5,000
Revised net worth	89,500	96,300	98,800
Revised capital gearing	81%	78%	74%
Clothing Imports Ltd:			
Actual borrowed money (as above)	108,000	122,000	157,000
Less: Directors' loans	10,000	10,000	10,000
Revised actual borrowed money	98,000	112,000	147,000
Net worth as above	80,000	96,000	98,000
Add: Directors' loans	10,000	10,000	10,000
Revised net worth	90,000	106,000	108,000
Revised capital gearing	109%	105%	136%

As can be seen, this amendment has had the effect of reducing the capital gearing ratio.

There is no straight answer as to whether directors' loans (or indeed other forms of quasi-capital, such as family loans which often occur in private companies) should be put on one side of the ratio or the other. It is down to a banker's judgment. That judgment, however, should be influenced by the *stability* of the loans. In the case of Clothing Imports Ltd, where the loan has been stable for three years, it would seem appropriate to regard the loan as supplementing shareholders' funds and, as such, including it in the net worth side of the equation.

(b) **Capital gearing adjusted for 'hidden reserves'**

In calculating the capital gearing ratio we have taken the *book value of the balance sheet assets.* These, for balance sheet purposes, are valued on a going-concern basis. Break-up valuations are considered later in this book, but we will consider at this point assets which we know have a different 'market' value.

In the case of companies where the bank has a first charge over the company's properties, the banker will have specific knowledge of the current value of these properties. For each of the two above companies, it is shown that the current value of the properties significantly exceeds the book value and, therefore, it would seem reasonable to adjust the net worth side of the ratio to properly reflect these 'hidden balance sheet reserves':

	19X4	19X5	19X6
Light Engineering Ltd:	£	£	£
Revised actual borrowed money (as (a) above)	72,500	75,000	72,900
Revised net worth (as (a) above)	89,500	96,300	98,800
Add: Current value less book value of property	10,000	15,000	20,000
Revised net worth	99,500	111,300	118,800
Revised capital gearing ratio	73%	67%	61%
Clothing Imports Ltd:			
Revised actual borrowed money (as (a) above)	98,000	112,000	147,000
Revised net worth (as (a) above)	90,000	106,000	108,000
Add: Current value less book value of property	24,000	24,000	24,000
Revised net worth	114,000	130,000	132,000
Revised capital gearing ratio	86%	86%	111%

If current valuation is less than book value then the difference should be deducted from net worth, which would increase the capital gearing ratio.

Hidden reserves may also occur in stock and work in progress but caution should be used in these circumstances, as such items are generally more difficult for a banker to value than freehold property.

(c) **Capital gearing adjusted for contingent liabilities**

The capital gearing ratio definition referred on the one side to actual borrowed money or actual usage of lines of credit. The two may not be identical. Actual borrowed money as revealed in a company's balance sheet will not include any usage of contingent liability facilities which the company may have. Such contingent liabilities may include documentary credits, indemnities, negotiated bills, forward exchange contracts, etc.

Whether these contingent liabilities should be included in the gearing ratio is open to question. On the one hand it could be argued that only interest-bearing liabilities should be included, in which case contingents could be ignored. On the other hand, before marking a contingent liability facility, a banker will certainly want to justify it against balance sheet strength, in which case it would seem appropriate to include them in the gearing ratio.

Many bankers adopt a sort of compromise. Whilst they include them as a liability in the ratio, they regard contingents as *'soft'* liability and, as a generality, will often be prepared to countenance higher gearing levels if the make-up of the ratio is substantially comprised of 'soft' liabilities.

By way of illustration let us assume that Light Engineering Ltd had no contingent liabilities outstanding, but that Clothing Imports Ltd had the following outstanding at its year ends.

	19X4	19X5	19X6
Irrevocable documentary credits	£40,000	£50,000	£60,000

Clothing Imports Ltd's capital gearing ratio can be further adjusted as follows:

	19X4	19X5	19X6
	£	£	£
Revised actual borrowed money (as (a) above)	98,000	112,000	147,000
Add: IDCs	40,000	50,000	60,000
Revised net worth (as (b) above)	114,000	130,000	132,000
Revised capital gearing ratio	121%	124%	156%

(d) **Potential capital gearing**

So far we have been calculating *actual* gearing. A banker will also need to consider the gearing position assuming full utilisation of whatever lines of credit are available, i.e., full potential gearing, in order to assess the full exposure to net worth.

The information given at the very beginning of the case study shows that total facilities marked by XYZ Bank as at end 19X6 for the two companies are:

Light Engineering Ltd	£78,000
Clothing Imports Ltd	£200,000

To this must be added hire-purchase commitments (it is assumed there are no undrawn hire-purchase credit lines) at 19X6 balance sheet date, i.e.:

Light Engineering Ltd	£78,000	+	£11,900	=	£89,900
Clothing Imports Ltd	£200,000	+	£9,000	=	£209,000

Revised net worth 19X6 (as (b) above)

Light Engineering Ltd	£118,800
Clothing Imports Ltd	£132,000

Potential gearing is thus:

Light Engineering Ltd $\frac{89,900}{118,800} \times 100 = 76\%$

Clothing Imports Ltd $\frac{209,000}{132,000} \times 100 = 158\%$

Caution It has been assumed that XYZ Bank are the sole bankers to both companies here. In considering potential gearing a Banker must make himself fully aware of any additional lines of credit that may be marked by other institutions, as such lines (even if undrawn) would have an impact on potential capital gearing. Even small companies can have contingent liability lines, such as IDCs, with banks other than their main bankers.

Capital gearing ratio summary

	19X4	19X5	19X6
Light Engineering Ltd	%	%	%
Actual capital gearing	91	91	83
Adjusted for directors' loans (a)	81	78	74
Further adjusted for 'hidden property reserve' (b)	73	67	61
(Contingent liabilities (c))	Not applicable		
Potential capital gearing (d)	Not available		76
Clothing Imports Ltd			
Actual capital gearing	135	127	160
Adjusted for directors' loans (a)	109	105	136
Further adjusted for 'hidden property reserve' (b)	86	86	111
Yet further adjusted for contingent liabilities (c)	121	124	156
Potential capital gearing (d)	Not available		158

The next ratio is an extension of the capital gearing ratio.

Total liabilities/net worth ratio

Before going on to comment on the interpretation of the trends seen so far, we need to consider this second ratio, which is defined as:

$$\frac{\text{Total liabilities (current + deferred)}}{\text{Net worth}} \times 100$$

For both companies we will use the net worth adjusted for directors' loans and hidden property reserves. The contingent liabilities outstanding for Clothing Imports Ltd will be included.

	19X4	19X5	19X6
Light Engineering Ltd	£	£	£
Current liabilities	54,000	69,200	60,500
Less: Directors' loans	4,500	6,500	5,000
	49,500	62,700	55,500
Add: Deferred liability	33,500	27,000	28,900
Total liabilities	83,000	89,700	84,400
Net worth (as (b) above)	99,500	111,300	118,800
Total liability/Net worth × 100	83%	81%	71%
Clothing Imports Ltd			
Current liabilities	250,000	307,000	435,000
Less: Directors' loans	10,000	10,000	10,000
	240,000	297,000	425,000
Add: Deferred liability	6,000	5,000	7,000
	246,000	302,000	432,000
Contingent liabilities (as (c) above)	40,000	50,000	60,000
Total liabilities	286,000	352,000	492,000
Net worth (as (b) above)	114,000	130,000	132,000
Total liability/Net worth × 100	251%	271%	372%

Interpretation of capital gearing and total liability/net worth ratios

We have calculated different measures of capital gearing and in addition the ratio between total liabilities and net worth. We must now consider what these ratios reveal. We have demonstrated that gearing ratios can be calculated in several different ways, and that the results can vary considerably. Before considering whether a ratio points to problems the banker must be fully aware of what is (or is not) included in either side of the ratios.

Ultimately the capacity of a company to service its debt from cash flow is a truer test than any capital gearing ratio. However, the higher the level of gearing, the less, proportionately, is the cushion of net worth before the lender's money is placed at risk.

The first thing to notice is the trend, Light Engineering Ltd's gearing ratios reveal a falling trend, suggesting that it is increasingly able to finance its operations. This is revealed also by the total liabilities/net worth ratio. In contrast, Clothing Imports Ltd shows a rising capital gearing trend, particularly in 19X6, implying greater reliance on borrowed funds to finance its increasing level of operations. Even more revealing is the huge rise in the total liability/net worth ratio. This latter ratio is really an extension of capital gearing. It can, and in this case does, reveal that, apart from borrowed money, the company is relying heavily on its creditors to finance its turnover. A steeply rising trend in this ratio can indicate that a company is undercapitalised and could be vulnerable if external liabilities are reduced due to factors beyond its control (e.g., creditors reducing terms of trade).

As mentioned earlier there is no simple mathematical formula to give a satisfactory gearing level; it's a matter of judgment. However, the banker will find it useful to bear the following points in mind:

(a) His judgment will be assisted by further ratio analysis, and a banker will generally feel happier with a highly geared situation if the customer has a long and profitable track record than if it is a new business or an old established one with a poor recent history of profit performance.

(b) Whether or not the banker is lending secured and what that security comprises are two important questions. Generally, the higher the gearing ratio, the more crucial becomes the quantity and quality of the security!

(c) What the gearing ratio comprises will be significant. If much of the borrowed money side of the ratio includes 'soft' contingent liabilities, high gearing levels are likely to be acceptable. Similarly with net worth — what is the asset structure? If the bulk of net worth is dependent upon stock or plant and machinery, the banker may feel less happy than if it comprised readily saleable freehold property. Also, is net worth heavily dependent on directors' loans which could easily be withdrawn? Overall, the banker must judge just how strong a buffer is that net worth before his own money is placed at risk.

(d) The type of business — this is crucial when assessing gearing levels. Generally speaking a wholesaler (such as Clothing Imports Ltd) can be expected to maintain and manage higher gearing levels than a manufacturer such as Light Engineering Ltd. Because of this a banker will often be more generous in lending (in gearing terms) to a wholesaler than to a manufacturer.

(e) The structure of the business — the banker may feel more comfortable in lending to a sole trader or partnership where there will be the addition of personal covenant, as opposed to a limited liability company.

(f) Light Engineering Ltd is quite highly geared for a manufacturer. Clothing Imports Ltd is certainly highly geared and the adverse trends are of concern. Whilst the security position suggests no immediate risk to the bank we shall need to look at other ratios carefully to build up a more complete picture.

INTEREST COVER

Interest cover can be measured on a historic profit basis by the ratio:

$$\frac{\text{Profit before interest and tax (PBIT)}}{\text{Interest paid}}$$

Light Engineering Ltd	19X4	19X5	19X6
PBIT / Interest paid	11,000 / 5,000	12,500 / 5,500	11,500 / 6,500
Interest cover (historic profit basis)	2.2:1	2.3:1	1.8:1

Clothing Imports Ltd	19X4	19X5	19X6
PBIT / Interest paid	33,000 / 8,000	34,500 / 8,500	13,000 / 11,000
Interest cover (historic profit basis)	4.1:1	4:1	1.2:1

The interest cover ratio tells us how many times interest paid is covered by profits before interest and tax. Obviously the higher the ratio the better. A ratio of 2:1 or less is considered low and can make a business vulnerable to fluctuations in interest rates. Also low cover has implications concerning the ability of a company to finance other areas of its business from retained profits and its ability to provide repayment of its debt from profits.

The interest cover ratios for Light Engineering Ltd look fairly tight for 19X4 and 19X5 and tight for 19X6. During 19X6 operating profits fell, whilst at the same time the company incurred higher interest charges.

As regards Clothing Imports Ltd, the interest cover ratio looked quite healthy up to and including 19X5. However, the decline in 19X6 gives cause for concern and if the trend were to continue the company would be unable to cover the interest on its debt for 19X7, let alone provide any repayment of its debt. Clearly the company has borrowed heavily in 19X6 to finance its increased turnover, but has failed to maintain its former profitability and former cash generation.

CONTROL RATIOS

Debtor recovery rate

This is defined as

$$\frac{\text{Debtors}}{\text{Sales}} \times 365$$

This ratio calculates the number of days taken to collect debts (debtor turnover).

Light Engineering Ltd	19X4	19X5	19X6
$\frac{\text{Debtor}}{\text{Sales}}$	$\frac{44{,}000}{200{,}000} \times 365$	$\frac{51{,}000}{220{,}000} \times 365$	$\frac{46{,}000}{210{,}000} \times 365$
Debt or recovery rate	80 days	85 days	80 days
Clothing Imports Ltd			
$\frac{\text{Debtors}}{\text{Sales}}$	$\frac{150{,}000}{900{,}000} \times 365$	$\frac{170{,}000}{1{,}050{,}000} \times 365$	$\frac{230{,}000}{1{,}300{,}000} \times 365$
Debt or recovery rate	60 days	59 days	65 days

Interpretation This ratio provides a 'rough and ready' indication of the efficiency of a company's credit control procedures. The length in days of the debtor recovery rate needs to be considered in the light of the company's terms of trade and those common for the sector in which the company operates. Obviously the debtor recovery rate should bear some resemblance to agreed terms of trade. The quicker the debt recovery rate the better, in so far as this will have a beneficial cash impact. Debtors are generally financed by bank overdraft and so minimising debtors by improving the debtor recovery rate will save interest charges and thus improve profits.

Perhaps more important than the absolute values of this ratio, is the trend that is revealed. A falling debtor recovery rate, i.e., a lengthening of credit given, could indicate:

(a) lax control by the invoicing department of the company;

(b) market competition which has forced a company to extend its terms of trade in order to maintain its sales outlets;

(c) slow paying and potential bad debts that may be included in the company's debtor book.

The above comments may lead you to believe that a trend that reveals a more rapid debtor recovery rate, i.e., a shortening of credit given, is always a good thing! A word of caution —

whilst a rapid recovery rate will have a beneficial effect on cash flow, it may have been caused by the company having to put pressure on its debtors because of cash flow problems. Too much pressure could result in a loss of future sales!

The golden rule is: ascertain by enquiry of the directors just what is causing a particular trend in the debtor recovery rate. Obtaining a full age analysis of debtors is worthwhile to give the full spread of debts (as indicated in Chapter 10).

As regards the two examples, in both cases the trends do not indicate any extreme variations.

Stock turnover rate

This is defined as

$$\frac{\text{Stock}}{\text{Cost of goods sold}} \times 365$$

This ratio indicates the number of days stock is held. (For simplicity's sake, in the following calculations, stock has been taken to include work in progress. However, it is often advisable to break the stock figure down into raw materials, finished goods and work in progress, and obtain separate ratios for each element in order to ascertain the stock component that underlies any particular trend.)

Light Engineering Ltd	19X4	19X5	19X6
$\frac{\text{Stock and WIP}}{\text{Cost of goods sold}}$	$\frac{35,000}{130,000} \times 365$	$\frac{44,000}{147,000} \times 365$	$\frac{40,000}{139,000} \times 365$
Stock turnover rate	98	109	105

Clothing Imports Ltd	19X4	19X5	19X6
$\frac{\text{Stock}}{\text{Cost of goods sold}}$	$\frac{135,000}{810,000} \times 365$	$\frac{190,000}{956,000} \times 365$	$\frac{257,000}{1,209,000} \times 365$
Stock turnover rate	61	72	77

Interpretation Ideally a rapid turnover is beneficial in that cash is tied up in stock for a shorter period. However, the optimum period of stock turnover will depend on the nature of that stock and the type of business concerned.

Again, trends are the thing to watch. A lengthening of the stock turnover rate may indicate obsolete items or damaged stocks that may ultimately be unsaleable. Also it is important to remember that stockholdings may be seasonal.

For Light Engineering Ltd, the ratio is reasonably static. A stock turnover of 100 days, i.e., over 3 months, should be considered, bearing in mind the greater proportion of stock lies in work in progress as opposed to 'items on the shelf'. As with all manufacturing companies, work in progress will depend on the length of time it takes to make an end product. This will vary depending on the type of product being manufactured.

The stock turnover for Clothing Imports Ltd is in many ways easier to comprehend, as all stock held will be finished goods awaiting a buyer or awaiting call-off from a firm order. A definite trend is being revealed here, and enquiry of the directors as to what underlies the trend is warranted. It may be that the stock includes unsaleable items caused by changes in fashion or stock that is out of season. Or it may merely represent the fact that the company is carrying more lines as a deliberate policy to back up increased sales.

Creditor repayment rate

This is defined as

$$\frac{\text{Creditors}}{\text{Cost of goods sold}} \times 365$$

This ratio indicates the number of days taken to pay creditors.

Light Engineering Ltd	19X4	19X5	19X6
$\frac{\text{Creditors}}{\text{Cost of goods sold}}$	$\frac{9,000}{130,000} \times 365$	$\frac{13,000}{147,000} \times 365$	$\frac{11,000}{139,000} \times 365$
Creditor repayment rate	25 days	32 days	29 days
Clothing Imports Ltd			
$\frac{\text{Creditors}}{\text{Cost of goods sold}}$	$\frac{140,000}{810,000} \times 365$	$\frac{180,000}{956,000} \times 365$	$\frac{280,000}{1,209,000} \times 365$
Creditor repayment rate	63 days	69 days	84 days

Interpretation As with debtor recovery rate, this ratio should be considered in the light of the terms of trade enjoyed by a business from its suppliers.

Again, it is trends that need to be analysed. Whilst lengthening this ratio will have a beneficial impact on cash flow, an escalating trend will usually imply problems — a company may be delaying payment to creditors because of cash flow problems. On the other hand, a shortening of this ratio may indicate concern on the part of creditors or a change in terms of trade from suppliers.

As regards Light Engineering Ltd, credit taken does not particularly indicate anything. Turning to Clothing Imports Ltd, the rising trend, particularly from 19X5 to 19X6, can be seen. Enquiry of the directors is appropriate here, to be supported by an age analysis of creditors. It appears the company has financed its expanding sales in part by taking longer credit. The bank facility of overdraft £138K + IDC usage £60K, against the agreed composite facility of £200K, may well mean that to maintain the overdraft usage within the agreed limit, the company has had no alternative but to delay paying creditors. By obtaining an age analysis of creditors the bank will be able to assess the problem more fully.

As a final comment under this ratio, care should be taken to establish just what the creditor figure comprises. Only trade creditors are relative to cost of goods sold. If possible, expense creditors (i.e., rates, power, PAYE and other sundry and tax creditors) should not be included in this ratio.

LIQUIDITY RATIOS

Current ratio and quick asset ratio

The current ratio is defined as

$$\frac{\text{Current assets}}{\text{Current liabilities}}$$

The quick asset ratio is defined as

$$\frac{\text{Quick assets (= Current assets less stock)}}{\text{Current liabilities}}$$

By their nature these two ratios can be looked at together.

The current ratio provides a measure of the ability of a business to meet its short-term liabilities from funds generated by current assets.

The quick asset ratio, by excluding stock from the comparison between current assets and current liabilities, expresses the cover for current liabilities in terms of cash or near cash (i.e. debtors). To that extent the quick asset ratio provides the more immediate measure of short-term liquidity.

Light Engineering Ltd	19X4	19X5	19X6
Current assets	80,000	96,000	86,000
Current liabilities	54,000	69,200	60,500
Current ratio	1.48:1	1.39:1	1.42:1
Quick assets	45,000	52,000	46,000
Current liabilities	54,000	69,200	60,500
Quick asset ratio	0.83:1	0.75:1	0.76:1

Clothing Imports Ltd	19X4	19X5	19X6
Current assets / Current liabilities	285,000 / 250,000	360,000 / 307,000	487,000 / 435,000
Current ratio	1.14:1	1.17:1	1.12:1
Quick assets / Current liabilities	150,000 / 250,000	170,000 / 307,000	232,000 / 435,000
Quick asset ratio	0.6:1	0.55:1	0.52:1

Interpretation Again the trend of the ratios needs to be examined. A falling trend in the current ratio, besides indicating a reducing ability to meet payments for current liabilities from current assets, may indicate reducing profit margins or losses. Also a reducing current ratio may arise from investment of liquid funds in fixed assets or alternatively borrowing on overdraft to finance fixed asset purchases.

Generally, the current and quick asset ratio should move in line. A static or increasing current ratio together with a falling quick ratio would indicate an increasing amount of money tied up in stockholding.

A surplus of current assets over current liabilities is a sign of good business liquidity.

Turning to the *example* case study, the ratios for Light Engineering Ltd have held up well. The quick asset ratio is less than 1:1 and so the company would be reliant on quickly translating work in progress into finished goods and then its debtors into cash in order to meet all its current liabilities.

Whilst the current ratio for Clothing Imports Ltd shows little movement, the quick asset ratio is revealing a declining trend. It should be recalled that both the stock turnover ratio and creditor repayment ratio were showing adverse trends — and the effect of this is borne out in the falling quick asset ratio. A picture is emerging of declining liquidity when measured by the quick asset ratio and lengthening of the creditor repayment and stock turnover ratios. Also in monetary values the gap is now considerable:

Quick assets	£230,000
Current liabilities	£435,000

Working capital turnover

This is defined as

$$\frac{\text{Sales}}{\text{Net current assets (working capital)}}$$

This ratio determines the relationship between sales and working capital.

Light Engineering Ltd	19X4	19X5	19X6
Sales / Net current assets	200,000 / 26,000	220,000 / 26,800	210,000 / 25,500
Working capital turnover	7.69:1	8.20:1	8.23:1
Clothing Imports Ltd			
Sales / Net current assets	900,000 / 35,000	1,050,000 / 53,000	1,300,000 / 52,000
Working capital turnover	25.71:1	19.81:1	25.00:1

Interpretation Again it is the trend that is important. A rising trend may indicate possible overtrading, whereby sales are increasing without the necessary additional working capital. Whilst a degree of overtrading can be often managed in the short term by good control over debtors, stock and creditors, over a period there will be increasing pressure on liquidity and the bank overdraft. As the ratio provides an indication of the working capital needed to finance a given level of sales, it can be used to calculate approximately the additional level of working capital required to finance a projected increase in sales.

The ratios for Light Engineering Ltd show a modest rising trend, but nothing significant.

Turning to Clothing Imports Ltd — the company increased its sales by 17% from 19X4 to 19X5. It can be seen that the ratio fell across this period. This has been possible by investing the retained profit into working capital to finance the sales expansion. From 19X5 to 19X6 sales expanded more rapidly, by 24%. This time the ratio has fallen back to its former level of 25:1. The nominal profit retention has not enabled the company to match its increased turnover.

This clearly has a bearing on liquidity, particularly if sales are projected to increase still further in 19X7. The company has already extended its credit taken, and unless stock turnover or credit given can be shortened, increased sales will necessitate still further reliance on creditors (which may not be possible) or increased bank borrowing (which may not be agreed).

By way of example, let us project forward on a further increase of 24%. The following ratios for 19X6 were applicable for Clothing Imports Ltd:

Debtor recovery rate	65 days
Stock turnover rate	77 days
Creditor repayment rate	84 days

Sales: £1,300,000 × 24% = £312,000 = increased sales
Total sales for 1987 = £1,612,000

If we further assume that the gross profit margin (see next section) for 19X7 will remain at 7%, gross profit = £113,000.

Therefore cost of goods sold = £1,499,000.

So applying a debtor recovery rate of 65 days to sales, projected debtors at 19X7 balance sheet date = (1,612,000/365) × 65 = £287,000.

And applying a stock turnover rate of 77 days to cost of goods sold, projected stock = (1,499,000/365) × 77 = £316,000.

Total projected current assets = £603,000.

How can this be financed?

Applying a creditor repayment rate of 84 days, projected creditors = (1,499,000 × 84)/365 = 344,000.

Assume other current liabilities, i.e., hire-purchase, tax and directors' loans remain the same: total £17,000.

Applying the 19X6 working capital

Turnover ratio to the projected sales level:

$$\frac{\text{£1,612,000}}{\text{Net current assets}} = 25$$

$$\text{Net current assets} = \frac{1{,}612{,}000}{25} = \text{£64,400}$$

Therefore projected bank overdraft at 19X7 year end is:

	£
Total projected current assets	603,000
Less: Projected creditors	344,000
Less: Other creditors	17,000
	242,000
Less: Projected net current assets	64,000
Projected bank overdraft	178,000

With this *rough* overdraft calculated, the bank then represents the 'balancing item' and this means a sizeable increased borrowing requirement which the bank may not be prepared to finance.

A second method This time we take out the bank balance from the working capital cycle and calculate

Debtors
plus Stock
minus Trade creditors

	19X4	19X5	19X6
	£	£	£
Debtors	150,000	170,000	230,000
Stock	135,000	190,000	257,000
	285,000	360,000	487,000
Trade creditors	140,000	180,000	280,000
Net balance	145,000	180,000	207,000
Sales	900,000	1,050,000	1,300,000
Net balance/sales	16%	17%	16%

This capital measure therefore equates approximately 16% of sales. The 19X7 sales are set to increase by £312,000.

The projected extra capital required:

£312,000 × 16% = £49,920

Although a gradual rise in profits will improve liquidity; this will not suffice and the bank will be needed as the 'balancing' item.

Note An alternative and more detailed method of demonstrating the bank requirement on an expanding sales profile is illustrated in Chapter 9 (see p. 118-127).

PROFITABILITY RATIOS

Gross profit margin

This is defined as

$$\frac{\text{Gross profit}}{\text{Sales}} \times 100$$

This ratio is calculated to show gross profit as a percentage of sales.

Light Engineering Ltd	19X4	19X5	19X6
$\frac{\text{Gross profit}}{\text{Sales}}$	$\frac{70,000}{200,000} \times 100$	$\frac{73,000}{220,000} \times 100$	$\frac{71,000}{210,000} \times 100$
Gross profit margin	35%	33%	34%

Clothing Imports Ltd	19X4	19X5	19X6
$\frac{\text{Gross Profit}}{\text{Sales}}$	$\frac{90{,}000}{900{,}000} \times 100$	$\frac{94{,}000}{1{,}050{,}000} \times 100$	$\frac{91{,}000}{1{,}300{,}000} \times 100$
Gross profit margin	10%	8.95%	7.0%

Interpretation This ratio will vary from business to business, e.g., a manufacturer with a high fixed cost structure will have a higher gross profit margin than a merchanting-type business (high volume—fine margin).

Trends in the gross profit margin should be noted carefully and the underlying reasons ascertained. A declining trend could indicate one or a combination of the following:

(a) The business is becoming less profitable due to competition in the market place forcing it to reduce its pricing policy.

(b) Similarly, it could be due to an increase in costs of one or more of the components of cost of goods sold, which the business cannot, due to competition, pass on to its customers.

(c) A deliberate policy by the business proprietors to reduce prices in order to increase sales volume.

Looking at Light Engineering Ltd, the gross profit margin fell from 35% to 33% from 19X4 to 19X5. Further analysis of the components of the cost of goods sold figures will show why:

	19X4	19X5
$\frac{\text{Materials consumed}}{\text{Sales}}$	$\frac{55{,}000}{200{,}000} \times 100$	$\frac{66{,}000}{220{,}000} \times 100$
Margin	27.5%	30%
$\frac{\text{Direct labour}}{\text{Sales}}$	$\frac{75{,}000}{200{,}000} \times 100$	$\frac{81{,}000}{220{,}000} \times 100$
Margin	37.5%	36.8%

Direct labour expressed as a percentage of sales actually fell, which in itself would boost the gross profit margin. However, it can be seen that this has been more than offset by an increase in materials consumed as a percentage of sales. An increase in materials costs then, relative to sales, has been the cause of the decline in the gross profit margin from 19X4 to 19X5.

During 19X6 the margin pulled back to 34%, reversing the trend. How was this achieved? A similar exercise to the above will enable the reader to demonstrate that comparing 19X6 with 19X5, direct labour costs increased as a percentage of sales. However, this was more than compensated for by a reduction in materials consumed as a percentage of sales.

Turning to Clothing Imports Ltd, a reducing trend can be seen, which is cause for concern. If this trend were to continue, and the gross profit margin fell by a further 1% in 19X7, on the same level of sales a gross profit as follows would be achieved:

Sales £1,300,000 × 6% = £78,000 gross profit.

Assuming similar fixed costs, i.e., administration and distribution costs of £78,000, the company would only break even. After interest charges a loss would be incurred.

It may be that the directors of Clothing Imports Ltd deliberately reduced gross margins to boost sales. Enquiries of the directors will need to be made to ascertain the reason behind the falling trend in gross margins.

Net profit margin

This is defined as

$$\frac{\text{Operating profit (PBIT)}}{\text{Sales}} \times 100$$

This ratio reveals the net margin before finance charges and tax.

Light Engineering Ltd	19X4	19X5	19X6
$\frac{\text{Operating profit}}{\text{Sales}}$	$\frac{11,000}{200,000} \times 100$	$\frac{12,500}{220,000} \times 100$	$\frac{11,500}{210,000} \times 100$
Net profit margin	5.5%	5.7%	5.5%

Clothing Imports Ltd	19X4	19X5	19X6
$\frac{\text{Operating Profit}}{\text{Sales}}$	$\frac{33,000}{900,000} \times 100$	$\frac{34,500}{1,050,000} \times 100$	$\frac{13,000}{1,300,000} \times 100$
Net profit margin	3.6%	3.3%	1.0%

Interpretation This ratio represents the premium gained by a business for its output over its production costs. Profit before interest and tax is used to isolate interest and tax charges from other costs of production. In interpreting the net profit margin it is important to observe any trend. The absolute value of the ratio will vary considerably from industry to industry, with low margins allied to high volume and vice versa. Variations in net margins from one year to another will be determined by variations in the gross profit and the overhead expenses. Having isolated the gross profit margin in the previous section, it is variations in the proportional expenses of overheads in relation to sales that will be revealed by an analysis of this ratio.

Looking at Light Engineering Ltd, it can be seen that the net profit margin is fairly steady.

Now turning to Clothing Imports Ltd, it can be seen that the net profit margin has fallen significantly during 19X6. This company has also sustained a steadily reducing gross profit margin. It is worthwhile ascertaining whether the two margins are reducing at the same rate. This is simply identified by the ratio:

$$\frac{\text{Net profit margin}}{\text{Gross profit margin}} \times 100$$

19X4	19X5	19X6
$\frac{3.6}{10} \times 100 = 36\%$	$\frac{3.3}{8.95} \times 100 = 36.87\%$	$\frac{1.0}{7.0} \times 100 = 14.28\%$

The two margins are not moving in line. We will concentrate on the greatest variation, i.e., 19X5 to 19X6, where net profit margin as a percentage of gross profit margin fell substantially. This must mean that there was a proportionate increase in overhead costs from 19X5 to 19X6. This can be ascertained by the following ratio:

$$\frac{\text{Overheads}}{\text{Sales}} \times 100$$

19X5	19X6
$\frac{59{,}500}{1{,}050{,}000} \times 100 = 5.66\%$	$\frac{78{,}000}{1{,}300{,}000} \times 100 = 6.0\%$

As well as a decline in gross margins, the fall in net profit margin in 19X6 was exacerbated by increased overhead costs.

Overall, the decline in gross profit margins, coupled with the decline in net profit margins for Clothing Imports Ltd, is cause for concern.

SOURCE AND APPLICATION OF FUNDS STATEMENT

Business failure usually occurs because of a cash crisis. It is important to appreciate that a cash crisis can occur even though a business is turning in profits. Such cash crises may be preceded by a series of funds flow deficits revealed in the source and application of funds statement.

Look again at the source and application of funds statements shown for the two companies in question:

* *Net funds generated (absorbed)* To what extent have the companies covered their tax payments and purchase of fixed assets from their own funds generated by operations?

* *Working capital change* If positive, can this be maintained? Increasing sales usually results in a need to increase working capital. Is working capital change 'swallowing up' all net funds generated by operations — as in 19X5 for both Light Engineering Ltd and Clothing Imports Ltd? Alternatively, is an increasing working capital requirement exacerbating an already deficit net funds generated position, as in 19X5 for Clothing Imports Ltd?

* *Cash funds deficit* How long will the business be able to continue to fund this from increased bank borrowing? Sooner or later a business may reach the limit of its creditworthiness.

SUMMARY ON RATIOS

What the ratios revealed and the interpretation of the trends seen form a guide to the financial health of the business being analysed. In assessing a business in this way it is important to appreciate that we are looking at *historical information*, but this assessment will enable the bank to have a *firm basis* upon which to consider future borrowing requirements. However, before the assessment can be complete, the bank will need to review the future corporate plan and forward projections of a business. These aspects will be considered in Chapters 8 and 9.

What did we glean from our ratio analysis?

Light Engineering Ltd

This company is maintaining its profitability on a *static* sales turnover. Its gearing position is improving, in part from retained profits, but also from increasing hidden balance sheet property reserves.

Liquidity and control ratios do not reveal anything untoward. The company's working capital position is not under any duress.

Overall, you may not be too concerned with present bank exposure. However, the company's future plans will need to be discussed. Will they be able to generate sufficient sales in 19X7 to maintain their position? Their 'bottom line' retained profits have been modest. There is little leeway if sales levels cannot be maintained. On the 'flat' sales turnover performance it is fortunate that they have been able to hold overhead costs at £60,000. A 10% rise in overheads on the same turnover would eliminate profits! Clearly much will depend on forecasts.

Clothing Imports Ltd

This company looks much more interesting! It has expanded its sales rapidly but only generated profit before tax of £2,000. The increased sales turnover has been accomplished only by reducing profit margins, and overall profitability has shown a marked decline.

The effect of the above has been to escalate capital gearing levels, particularly the wider measure of total liabilities/net worth. Gearing is high and so the bank's margin of safety rests very heavily on the security cover. Interest cover has declined.

Liquidity has declined — with the company having to extend its credit taken to finance its increased sales levels. Working capital requirements are under some strain. The company will not be able to expand sales at the same rates as in these three years without increasing its bank borrowing and/or credit taken.

Overall, the directors' strategy for 19X6 need questioning, together with their forward plans and budgets for 19X7. Do they realise the cash flow implications of another year of growth similar to that seen in 19X6?

8 Serviceability

We will now consider serviceability, and will leave our corporate structure for the moment and look at a sole-trader.

As stated earlier, serviceability is a very important aspect in banking. It is not sufficient to justify the bank advance with asset cover and security — we must also look at the *business's capacity to meet its commitments and service its borrowing.*

This aspect is, of course, applicable to *any* business, but as an illustration we will take a farming case study. This sector traditionally provides strong asset cover, which can result in a low gearing position, but there may well be servicing difficulties.

In assessing a farmer's capacity to meet his commitments and service his borrowing, as well as looking at the past profit records and trends in net worth, examination of farm enterprise recordings is useful to see more up-to-date progress. For example, a dairy farmer could be recording his dairy herd on a Milk Marketing Board scheme or ICI Dairymaid scheme. Figures will be available, usually up to the end of the previous month, in a very detailed analysis of input costs and output (per cow) for all the herd — identified only by code number — in his area. Examination will indicate not only month by month costs and output, but also 'rolling' averages, i.e., annual averages updated month by month.

QUICK GUIDELINES FOR SERVICEABILITY

There are two methods which will quickly identify the financial pressures that the farm business will face.

Rent and finance charges (rental equivalent)

This is useful as a guideline for tenant and owner-occupiers or a combination of both. It takes into account *all financial commitments* plus the rent payable, and thereby removes the distinction between the tenant and owner. It is very useful to discuss this with the farmer, who usually has a 'gut feeling' as to the level of rental equivalent per acre that he can cope with successfully. The figure is calculated by including the following charges *per annum*:

(a) rent and rates;
(b) bank overdraft interest;
(c) bank loans, capital repayments and interest;
(d) Agricultural Mortgage Corporation — interest and capital repayment;

(e) hire-purchase charges;
(f) leasing charges;
(g) merchant credit charges;
(h) private loans — interest and capital.

This total is then divided by the effective acreage (i.e., the total *productive* land area).

The interpretation of this rental equivalent depends on the type of the farm and farming system. As a general guide, £80 per acre is often talked of as a figure below which servicing should not be too difficult. Above £80 per acre needs a closer look. This is only a general guideline — so be careful!

It is advisable to build up your own file on rental equivalents. The author carried this out in Sussex in 1982, and in the table below the variations which occur between different types of farm become more apparent. The figures are now somewhat historic but they do illustrate the point:

Survey of rental equivalents

Farm type	Average size (acres)	Break-even rental equivalent per acre Average £	High £
Cereal farm	450	53	79
Dairy farm	260	50	76
Cereals/Dairy	600	44	73
Beef/Sheep	300	37	51
Arable	700	57	97

These break-even figures suggest, for example, that an average cereal farmer on 450 acres could cope with a maximum rental equivalent of £53 per acre whereas a good farmer could cope with £79 per acre. For a beef/sheep farmer, the corresponding figures are £37 and £51. Thus the rental equivalent figure is only a quick reference guideline in assessing the likely financial pressure.

Rental equivalent as a percentage of gross output (REGO)

The rental equivalent yardstick takes no account of the output of the business but this second measurement looks at rental equivalent as a percentage of farm gross output. The farm gross output is a net of total farm returns *plus* the value of produce consumed in the farmhouse or supplied to workers, *less* purchases of livestock and other products bought for resale.

Guidelines are:

Less than 10% — there should be little problem
Between 10% and 15% is the usual range
15%-20% is getting tighter and needs a closer look
20% or more is considered high

BUDGETS

The guidelines we have looked at, i.e., rental equivalent and rental equivalent as a percentage of gross output, are only quick measurements. The total serviceability picture can be seen far more clearly when examining the total farm budget. Some farmers argue that budgets are a waste of time to which the answer is that any budget is better than none! They are certainly essential in planning the profitability of the farm.

If the farmer cannot prepare farm budgets himself there are many people prepared to assist. The first point of reference is the Ministry of Agriculture's Agricultural Development and Advisory Service (ADAS), which has offices throughout the country. There is also the Milk Marketing Board, ICI, and the Meat and Livestock Commission, and certain firms of accountants — all have advisers trained to help the farmer. Some commercial suppliers of fertilisers, feedstuffs, etc., also have specialist advisory services.

ADAS will also give the farmer detailed technical advice on land usage, enterprises, soil analysis, suitability of buildings, grants available, and classified results for comparison with individual farms. The ADAS adviser will also help with the completion of cash flow forecasts and capital expenditure budgets if required. All the advisers use the same gross margin techniques for farm budgets and although the layout may differ, provided you understand gross margins you should be able to understand any farm budget presented to you.

For example: 1 acre winter wheat

			£
Gross output: 2.75 tons @ £110		=	302
Less: Variable costs			
Seed Fertiliser Spray	say		82
Gross margin			220

CASE STUDY: FARMER C (Reproduced from the author's *Finance for Farming,* Chartered Institute of Bankers, 1982)

This case study is being used again because the principles are still very relevant. It also continues our capital gearing theme but this time with a low gearing of 58%.

Farmer C is an owner-occupier of 242 acres. This is his balance sheet:

Farmer C: Balance sheet

Liabilities	£	Assets	£
Rent outstanding	—	Cash at bank	—
Due to bank:		Debtors	500
Current account	84,510	Grants due	—
Loan account	—	Stock:	
Creditors	5,000	Produce for sale	
Hire-purchase	—	Livestock	8,280
Private loans (short-term)	—	Produce for own consumption	—
		Fertilizer/seed/feed etc.	6,220
Sub total	89,510	Valuation:	
Mortgages (AMC)	70,100	Growing crops	14,630
Dilapidations	—	Tenant right	—
Other liabilities	—		
		Sub total	29,630
Liabilities	159,610	Land & buildings	
		242 acres @ £1,500	363,000
		Farm machinery	29,300
		Tenant's improvements	—
Date:			
Net worth/balance	262,320		
	421,930	Total	421,930

Other items:

(1) Contingent liabilities: Nil
(2) Leasing: Nil
(3) Non-farming assets: Life policy — surrender value £3,150

A first cursory glance at Farmer C's balance sheet would seem to reveal no problem:

Total assets	£421,930 (capital gearing 58%)
Total liabilities	£159,610
Net worth	£262,320

However, this farmer is unable to service his finance costs. His current liabilities far exceed his current asets. A farm budget reveals the following:

Farmer C: Gross margin budget

			£	£
200 ewes		@	33.5	6,700
90 acres winter wheat		@	185.5	16,700
50 acres winter barley		@	153	7,650
35 acres winter oats		@	167	5,845
Total farm gross margins				36,895
Less: fixed costs:	£			
Labour	3,500			
Farm machinery:				
running	6,900			
replacement (depreciation)	5,210			
Other costs	6,080			
				21,690
Trading margin				15,205
To meet finance costs: total*	21,700			
Plus: Drawings	6,000			
				27,700
Negative margin				12,495

Rental equivalent: £90 per acre

Rental equivalent as % of gross output (say 57,500) = 37%

*Bank O/D (say) £70,000 @ 15%: £10,500
AMC (20-year loan): £11,200

Farmer C is in a strong position in asset terms. He can sell a parcel of land to make a capital injection. However, before taking any action at all, this case needs some urgent attention by Farmer C's accountant.

Detailed profit and loss figures must be produced quickly to pinpoint the exact situation. Also, tax computations will need to be made to ascertain the amount of fixed assets to be sold or sold and leased back. It certainly looks as though some action is needed to reduce the financial burden. Enterprise improvements will only have a minimal effect unless the farm enterprises can be changed to achieve significantly higher output, coupled with the same level of fixed costs or, better still, a lower level.

BREAK-EVEN ANALYSIS

The separation of farming costs into fixed and variable makes graphic presentation straightforward. In using breakeven charts the link between variable costs and output is easily seen and the point of minimum output for the business to service its borrowing is shown (see Figure 1). This technique is useful when trying to illustrate the vulnerability of a particular farm business, i.e., when the margin of safety is slight or even non-existent.

The simple chart in Figure 1 assumes an an even spread of sales income over the year. In this case the break-even point is £30,000 farm output. There is a good margin of safety.

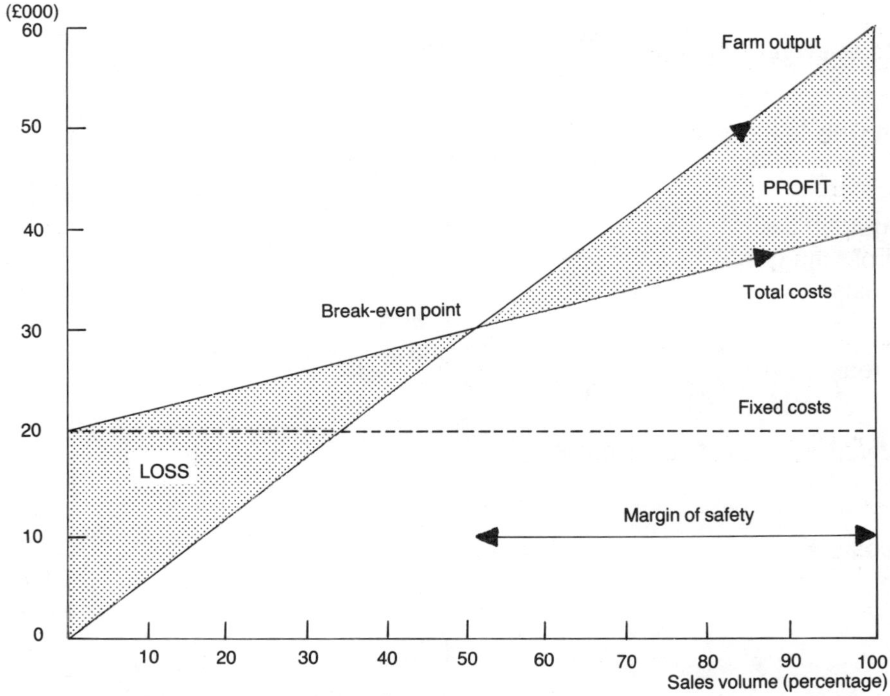

Farm output: £60,000; Variable costs: £20,000; Fixed costs: £20,000

Figure 1 Break-even chart

Alternatively, break-even can be calculated arithmetically. Using the figures from the chart:

	£
Farm output	60,000
Less: Variable cost	20,000
Farm gross margin	40,000
Less: Fixed costs	20,000
Trading margin	20,000

Therefore

$$\frac{\text{Fixed costs}}{\text{Gross margin \%}} = \frac{\pounds 20{,}000}{66.67\%} = 30{,}000 \text{ (= break-even point)}$$

This may also be expressed as

$$\text{Break-even output} = \text{Fixed cost} \times \frac{\text{Farm output}}{\text{Farm gross margin}}$$

Using the above figures

$$\text{Break-even} = 20{,}000 \times \frac{60{,}000}{40{,}000} = \pounds 30{,}000$$

Applying this to Farmer C's case:

	£
Gross output	57,500
Total gross margin	36,895 (64.2%)
Fixed costs	21,690

$$\text{Break-even} = \frac{\text{Fixed costs}}{\text{Gross margin \%}} = \frac{21{,}690}{64.2\%} = \pounds 33{,}785$$

However, if we add in finance costs:

	£
Fixed costs =	21,690 +
	21,700
	43,390

$$\text{Break-even} = \frac{43{,}390}{64.2\%} = \pounds 67{,}585$$

Therefore the output of the business would need to increase by £10,000 before Farmer C would even break even.

This again illustrates the limitation of looking at capital gearing in isolation — it is important to carry out further research to demonstrate serviceability.

CASE STUDY: FARMER D

Let us examine another example and this time incorporate *budget flexing* to see if we can achieve serviceability.

Farmer D is a successful farmer with £500,000 placed on bank deposit account. He has been in farming for many years and knows the local land to such an extent that any financial backer should be confident in his ability to farm.

There is a 500 acre farm coming up for sale. How much capital will Farmer D need to buy and farm it? It will depend on, firstly, the land price and, secondly, the working capital requirements of the planned farm enterprise structure.

Assume the following:

	£
£1,600 per acre land cost	800,000
£400 per acre tenants assets	200,000
Total capital required	1,000,000

If the bank will match Farmer D's stake of £500,000 with £500,000 borrowing then the proposal will be fully secured by the land and will be geared at 1:1 (net worth:debt).

The formation farmer's balance sheet in simple summary will be:

	£000		£000
Bank	500	Tenants assets	200
Capital	500	Land	800
	1,000		1,000

You could consider the gearing satisfactory in view of the security of the land. A banker would be safe; but can Farmer D service this level of borrowing at a budgeted interest rate of, say, 15%?

Let us run the same serviceability checks as we did with the previous farming case study.

Rental equivalent

You will recall that this is the total of rent plus finance charges divided by the *effective* acreage.

The proposal was for:

	£000
Rent	—
Finance (£500k @ 15%)	75
Total	75

£75,000 divided by 500 = £150 per acre.

This is a high level of charge.

Rental equivalent as a percentage of gross output

In order to calculate this we must first obtain the gross output figures for the farm based on the planned enterprise structure which has been selected for the farm:

120 dairy cows rearing replacements
200 acres of winter wheat
100 acres of spring barley

(Ignore current milk quota implications for the moment — we will come back to this later.)

Gross output has been calculated as follows:

	£
Milk sales	98,160
Cull cows/surplus calf sales	33,045
Cereal sales	77,217
Total	208,422

We can now calculate rental equivalent as a % gross output:

$$\frac{75,000}{208,422} \times 100 = 36\%$$

Gross margin budget

The next step in our case study is to build up a gross margin budget:

Gross margin budget

Enterprise		Gross margin	Total
		£	£
120 dairy cows	@	448	53,760
30 dairy replacements	@	238	7,140
200 acres winter wheat	@	194	38,800
100 acres spring barley	@	134	13,400
Total farm gross margin			113,100
Less: Fixed Costs:		£	
Labour		27,444	
Power and machinery:			
Running costs		22,223	
Replacement costs		18,038	
Rent and rates		1,000	
Other costs		10,310	79,015
Trading margin			34,085
Less: Finance costs			
O/D interest			75,000
			(40,915)
Less: Drawings			5,000
			(45,915)

Comments It is not necessary to worry too much about the individual gross margins. The purpose is to illustrate the layout of this type of budget. This gross margin budget clearly illustrates a huge shortfall of £45,915 after minimal drawings. The farm business has a *positive trading margin* of £34,085 from a total farm gross margin of £113,100 less fixed costs of £79,015, but this is insufficient to meet the finance costs of £75,000.

Before we consider flexing the budget we will look at the likely cash flow requirements.

Cash flow

	£
Total projected cash receipts are	208,422
Total projected payments are	156,135
Net cash flow	+52,287

Comments The problem is that we have to pay interest charges on £75,000, plus drawings, plus any machinery purchased and other capital items out of £52,287 of positive cash flow. In this example we are paying *interest only* — if we are also to build in a loan repayment schedule then it would be worse still!

Cash flow budget

	Jun £	Jul £	Aug £	Sep £	Oct £	Nov £	Dec £	Jan £	Feb £	Mar £	Apr £	May £	Total
Milk sales	7,853	8,834	6,871	5,890	6,871	6,871	7,853	8,834	7,853	9,816	10,798	9,816	98,160
Cull cows/calf sales	0	0	0	2,801	4,630	4,794	4,465	4,794	4,794	4,794	1,973	0	33,045
Cereal sales	0	0	0	0	11,607	17,386	17,386	13,501	11,558	5,779	0	0	77,217
Total income	7,853	8,834	6,871	8,691	23,108	29,051	29,704	27,129	24,205	20,389	12,771	9,816	208,422
Livestock purchases	0	0	0	808	2,430	2,450	2,410	2,450	2,450	2,450	241	0	15,689
Feed—cows	1,922	1,922	1,922	1,922	2,563	2,884	3,204	3,524	3,524	3,845	2,884	1,922	32,038
Feed—cattle	0	0	0	288	360	432	540	540	540	540	360	0	3,600
Fertilisers	0	7,029	0	0	0	0	0	0	0	11,667	0	1,912	20,608
Seed	0	0	101	3,642	0	0	0	0	0	1,497	570	0	5,810
Sprays	0	0	0	2,914	0	0	0	0	0	5,828	251	168	9,161
Vet. med.	1,050	0	0	1,050	0	0	1,050	0	0	1,050	0	0	4,200
Other costs	0	0	1,013	0	0	1,013	0	0	1,013	0	0	1,013	4,052
Total variable costs	2,972	8,951	3,036	9,816	2,923	4,329	4,794	4,064	5,077	24,427	4,065	5,015	79,469
Labour	2,196	2,196	2,470	2,744	2,744	2,470	1,920	1,921	1,929	2,196	2,470	2,196	27,444
Power & machinery running	1,778	1,778	2,000	2,222	2,222	2,000	1,555	1,556	1,556	1,778	2,000	1,778	22,223
Rent and rates	0	0	0	0	500	0	0	0	0	0	500	0	1,000
Other costs	859	859	859	859	859	859	861	859	859	859	859	859	10,310
Total fixed costs	4,833	4,833	5,329	5,825	6,325	5,329	4,336	4,336	4,336	4,833	5,829	4,833	60,977
Total payments	7,805	13,784	8,365	16,449	11,678	12,108	11,540	10,850	11,863	31,710	10,135	9,848	156,135
Net cash flow	48	−4,950	−1,494	−7,758	11,430	16,943	18,164	16,279	12,342	−11,321	2,636	−32	52,287

Flexing the budget

The benefit of having obtained a budget on a gross margin basis (or an industrial profit budget — see next case study), is that we can ask ourselves 'What if . . . ?' In other words, can performance levels be flexed to achieve viability?

Returning to our gross margin budget, what can we do? First we will recalculate the budget figures based on a *good* farm performance.

Gross margin budget (2)

Enterprise		Gross margin £	Total £
120 dairy cows	@	490	58,800
30 dairy replacements	@	259	7,770
200 acres winter wheat	@	225	45,000
100 acres spring barley	@	151	15,100
Total farm gross margin			126,670
Less: Fixed costs:			
Labour		27,444	
Power and machinery:			
Running costs		22,223	
Replacement costs		18,038	
Rent and rates		1,000	
Other costs		10,310	79,015
Trading margin		47,655	
Less: Finance costs			
O/D interest			75,000
			(27,345)
Less: Drawings			5,000
			(32,345)

It can be seen by comparing this second gross margin budget with the previous one that, although the trading margin has improved by £13,570 (£47,655 – £34,085) *we are still £32,345 negative* after minimal drawings.

Examining both budgets, the interest rate at 15% is obviously a key factor. If we dropped it to 10% then £500,000 @ 10% = £50,000 interest and our second gross margin budget would just about work. However, that was for a good farmer and also a base rate of below 10% to give an effective charging rate of 10%.

Restructuring

What else can we do? Let's restate our enterprises and contributions gained:

Enterprises	Gross margin £	Total £
120 dairy cows	490	58,800
30 dairy replacements	259	7,770
200 acres winter wheat	225	45,000
100 acres spring barley	151	15,100
		126,670

Examining the gross margins on a pound for pound contribution analysis basis, we could consider running a 'flying herd' (no herd replacements) and building up the cow numbers to fully stock the 200 acres of grass with dairy cows (ignoring milk quotas).

Gross margin budget (3)

Restructured enterprises		Gross margin £	Total £
162 dairy cows	@	490	79,380
200 acres winter wheat	@	225	45,000
100 acres spring barley	@	151	15,100
Total farm gross margin			139,480
Less: Fixed costs:			
Labour		29,558	
Power and machinery:			
Running costs		23,935	
Replacement costs		19,427	
Rent and rates		1,000	
Other costs		11,104	85,024
Trading margin			54,456
Less: Finance costs			
O/D interest			75,000
			(20,544)
Less: Drawings			5,000
			(25,544)

Comments From the third gross margin budget we see an improvement to the farm gross margin by £12,810 (£139,480 – £126,670). However, this is eroded by more labour and machinery costs incurred in carrying the increased dairy herd. The trading margin does show a net improvement of nearly £7,000 but we are still £25,544 short at the budgeted interest rate of 15%.

Also we would need to consider the additional net capital cost of buying in 42 dairy cows at say £600/£700 each (£27,000) less funds realised by selling off surplus young stock.

Second restructuring

Let's have a final try! This time Farmer D will put down to grass an additional 100 acres previously in wheat, again carry no dairy followers (i.e., have a 'flying herd') and (ignoring milk quotas) run 243 dairy cows. Again, he is a good farmer.

Gross margin budget (4)

Enterprises		Gross margin £	Total £
243 dairy cows	@	490	119,070
100 acres winter wheat	@	225	22,500
100 acres spring barley	@	151	15,100
Total farm gross margin			156,670
Less: Fixed costs:			
Labour		37,099	
Power and machinery			
Running costs		27,921	
Replacement costs		19,886	
Rent and rates		1,000	
Other costs		14,804	100,710
Trading margin			55,960
Less: Finance costs			
O/D interest			75,000
			(19,040)
Less: Drawings			5,000
			(24,040)

Comments We are still short but the point is now clear that although the capital gearing in both the farming case studies may well be considered at a satisfactory level, we need to take care to ensure serviceability.

The figures were for hypothetical farms but the format used will apply to any type of farming business.

9 Liquidity

This is an area of vital importance for all businesses. We looked briefly at this very important aspect in our earlier case study Clothing Imports Ltd. We will restate the most recent year's figures (19X6) to refresh your memory on the company's performance and ratios:

Profit and loss account 19X6

		£
Sales		1,300,000
Materials consumed	1,209,000	
Direct labour	—	1,209,000
Gross profit		91,000
Admin. and distribution expenses		78,000
Operating profit		13,000
Interest paid		11,000
Profit before tax		2,000
Tax		—
Attributable profit after tax		2,000

Balance sheet: 19X6

	£
Cash	—
Debtors	230,000
Quick assets	230,000
Stock	257,000
Total current assets	487,000
Creditors	280,000
Hire-purchase	2,000
Bank	138,000
Tax	5,000
Directors' loans	10,000
Total current liabilities	435,000
Net current assets	52,000
Property at cost	36,000
Net current value	(60,000)
Machinery and plant	3,000
Fixtures and fittings	4,000
Motor vehicles	10,000
Total fixed assets	53,000
Bank loans	—
Long-term HP	7,000
Total deferred liabilities	7,000
Net tangible assets	98,000
Share capital	20,000
P & L account	78,000
Shareholders' funds	98,000

Source and application of funds statement: 19X6

Source of funds:		£
Profit before tax		2,000
Depreciation		2,000
Funds generated by operations	(A)	4,000
Application of funds:		
Purchase of fixed assets		7,000
Tax paid		5,000
	(B)	12,000
Net funds generated (absorbed) (A-B)	(C)	(8,000)
Working capital change*	(D)	(27,000)
Funds available for repayment of bank and HP liabilities (C-D)		(35,000)
Increase (decrease) in long-term debt		2,000
Increase (decrease) in net short-term debt		33,000
		35,000

*Working capital change:	
Increase (decrease) in creditors	100,000
Less: Increase (decrease) in debtors	60,000
Less: Increase (decrease) in stock	67,000
	(27,000)

We considered earlier how the company's expanding business could be financed.

What areas of *any* expanding business need financing?

* Debtors
* Stock
* Work in progress
* Fixed assets

Where are these funds likely to come from?

* Bank
* Increased creditors
* Hire-purchase
* Loans
* New capital
* Retained profit

SOURCE AND APPLICATION OF FUNDS STATEMENT

The *basic* points listed above form the foundation of the document known as the source and application of funds statement. This is defined by SSAP 10 as

> A statement that shows the movements in assets, liabilities and capital that have taken place over any period in question and the result and effect on net liquid funds.

The table below analyses 'what goes where' in the statement:

Sources	*Uses*
Bank	Debtors
Creditors	Stock
Hire-purchase	Work in progress
Loans	Fixed assets
New capital	
Retained profit	
Decreases in an asset	Increases in an asset
Profit from operations (after adding back non-funds items, e.g., depreciation)	Loss from operations (after adding back depreciation etc.)
Increase in a liability	Decrease in a liability
Increase in equity	Decrease in equity

This type of analysis is also very useful to *project* the funds requirement forward for a business. By building on to profit and cash budgets we can project forward anticipated levels of stock, debtors, creditors, etc.

Financial sources, e.g., bank, hire-purchase, leasing, can then be considered as a balancing item. This type of analysis will help with assessing whether or not to go ahead with a particular project.

Examination of the funds flow documentation will show us funds utilised to provide working capital and funds utilised to purchase fixed assets. Also analysis will show the source of the funds — whether long-term or short-term.

THE WORKING CAPITAL CYCLE

This is the length of time between the outlay of cash for materials and the inflow of cash from sales. It is often shown diagramatically, as in Figure 1.

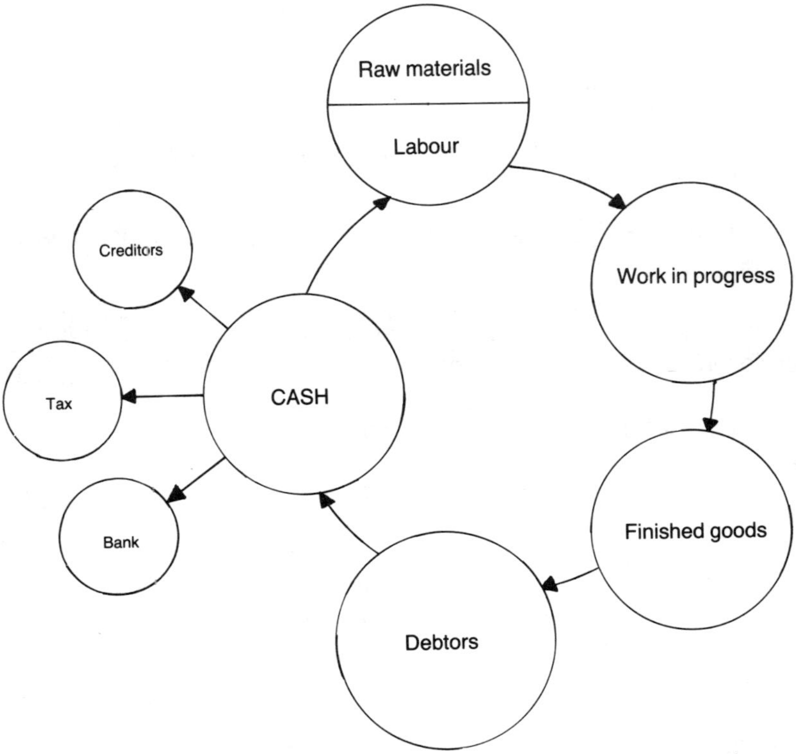

Figure 1 Working capital cycle

Look again at the *working capital movements* for Clothing Imports Ltd in 19X6:

	£
Increase in debtors	60,000
Increase in stock	67,000
	127,000

This was sourced primarily from trade creditors and the bank.

FINANCING EXPANSION PLANS

The 19X6 performance figures must be discussed with Clothing Imports Ltd's directors, expressing concern at the following:

(a) Despite sales increasing by 24%, net profit is minimal at £2,000.
(b) The gross profit margin has fallen to 7%.
(c) Gearing has deteriorated.
(d) Working capital looks under strain with both the bank and trade creditors increased from 19X5 levels.

The directors reply that sales for 19X7 are projected at £2.6 million (double the 19X6 turnover), and by holding overhead costs they are expecting to make a net profit of about £90,000.

The bank responds by commenting that although the profit sounds very attractive, have the directors fully considered the working capital implications of such an expansion plan. A request is made for some detailed figures to be prepared, with the help of their accountant if necessary.

The figures they produce are:

(a) profit budget;
(b) cash flow forecast;
(c) flow of funds statement.

Clothing Imports Ltd: Profit budget (I)

	Jan	Feb	Mar	Apr	May	Jun	Jul	Aug	Sep	Oct	Nov	Dec	Total
	£	£	£	£	£	£	£	£	£	£	£	£	£
Forecast sales	160,000	180,000	260,000	280,000	180,000	120,000	180,000	240,000	360,000	260,000	220,000	160,000	2,600,000
	160,000	180,000	260,000	280,000	180,000	120,000	180,000	240,000	360,000	260,000	220,000	160,000	2,600,000
Forecast purchases	162,540	185,060	269,300	288,100	185,200	123,400	185,200	246,800	370,300	263,600	220,400	169,236	2,669,136
Stock change	−13,740	−17,660	−27,500	−27,700	−17,800	−11,800	−17,800	−23,600	−35,500	−21,800	−15,800	−20,436	−251,136
Total direct costs	148,800	167,400	241,800	260,400	167,400	111,600	167,400	223,200	334,800	241,800	204,600	148,800	2,418,000
Gross profit	11,200	12,600	18,200	19,600	12,600	8,400	12,600	16,800	25,200	18,200	15,400	11,200	182,000
Less:													
Revenue payments	6,500	6,500	6,500	6,500	6,500	6,500	6,500	6,500	6,500	6,500	6,500	6,500	78,000
Monthly interest	1,128	1,131	940	745	532	358	730	1,307	1,400	1,155	720	791	10,937
Trading profit	3,572	4,969	10,760	12,355	5,568	1,542	5,370	8,993	17,300	10,545	8,180	3,909	93,063

(All figures rounded to nearest pound)

Clothing Imports Ltd: Cash flow forecast 19X7 (I)

	Jan	Feb	Mar	Apr	May	Jun	Jul	Aug	Sep	Oct	Nov	Dec	Total
	£	£	£	£	£	£	£	£	£	£	£	£	£
Sales receipts	106,154	106,154	171,026	203,167	283,667	318,167	226,167	149,500	195,500	264,500	391,000	318,167	2,733,167
Total receipts	106,154	106,154	171,026	203,167	283,667	318,167	226,167	149,500	195,500	264,500	391,000	318,167	2,733,167
Purchase payments	100,000	100,000	117,384	192,101	232,194	314,019	307,648	198,766	156,124	227,148	312,225	401,304	2,658,913
Revenue payments	6,500	6,500	6,500	6,500	6,500	6,500	6,500	6,500	6,500	6,500	6,500	6,500	78,000
Overdraft interest	0	0	3,200	0	0	1,635	0	0	3,437	0	0	2,665	10,937
VAT	0	0	0	−2,535	0	0	−2,505	0	0	−3,345	0	0	−8,385
Total payments	106,500	106,500	127,084	196,066	238,694	322,154	311,643	205,266	166,061	230,303	318,725	410,469	2,739,465
Net cash flow	−346	−346	43,942	7,101	44,973	−3,987	−85,476	−55,766	29,439	34,197	72,275	−92,302	−6,299
Opening bank balance	−138,000	−138,346	−138,692	−94,751	−87,650	−42,677	−46,665	−132,141	−187,907	−158,468	−124,271	−51,996	
Closing bank balance	−138,346	−138,692	−94,751	−87,650	−42,677	−46,665	−132,141	−187,907	−158,468	−124,271	−51,996	−144,299	

(All figures rounded to nearest pound)

Clothing Imports Ltd: Flow of funds statement 19X7 (I)

Source:	£	Application:	£
Deterioration in bank balance	6,299	Increase in debtors	256,833
Increase in creditors	408,608	Increase in stock	251,136
Net profit (before depreciation)	93,063		
	507,969		507,969

End of year liquid figures

Liabilities:	£	Assets:	£
Bank debit balance	144,299	Trade debtors	486,833
Trade creditors	690,593	Closing stock	508,136
Accrued VAT	−1,985		
Accrued interest	0		

Comments on forecasts (I) Sales are forecast at £2.6 million, resulting in a gross profit of £182,000 (7%). With overheads at £78,000 (as in 19X6), this results in a significant net profit of £93,000.

However, the cash flow implications of this plan must be considered. The cash flow (I) reveals a peak position in August of £187,907 but falling back to a similar position to the opening balance. The increase, then, would 'only' be £50,000 on the bank requirement to double the sales turnover.

How has the company managed that? The expansion has been financed on the back of the trade creditors — see flow of funds statement (I). The end of the year figures clearly illustrate that the burden of finance is now with trade credit and stands at £690,593!

Questions we must ask now are:

* Will the suppliers go along with this level of credit for a company with 19X6 net worth of £98,000 and generating only very modest profits?

* Should the bank back this planned expansion?

Before deciding, let us suppose that the trade creditors stipulate a maximum trade line of, say, £500,000. What effect will that have on the bank account? This is shown by forecasts (II).

Profit budget (II)

	Jan £	Feb £	Mar £	Apr £	May £	Jun £	Jul £	Aug £	Sep £	Oct £	Nov £	Dec £	Total £
Forecast sales	160,000	180,000	260,000	280,000	180,000	120,000	180,000	240,000	360,000	260,000	220,000	160,000	2,600,000
	160,000	180,000	260,000	280,000	180,000	120,000	180,000	240,000	360,000	260,000	220,000	160,000	2,600,000
Forecast purchases	162,540	185,060	269,300	288,100	185,200	123,400	185,200	246,800	370,300	263,600	220,400	169,236	2,669,136
Stock change	−13,740	−17,660	−27,500	−27,700	−17,800	−11,800	−17,800	−23,600	−35,500	−21,800	−15,800	−20,436	−251,136
Total direct costs	148,800	167,400	241,800	260,400	167,400	111,600	167,400	223,200	334,800	241,800	204,600	148,800	2,418,000
Gross profit	11,200	12,600	18,200	19,600	12,600	8,400	12,600	16,800	25,200	18,200	15,400	11,200	182,000
Less:													
Revenue payments	6,500	6,500	6,500	6,500	6,500	6,500	6,500	6,500	6,500	6,500	6,500	6,500	78,000
Monthly interest	1,128	1,131	1,840	2,769	3,119	2,685	2,202	2,289	3,416	4,636	4,627	3,685	33,527
Trading profit	3,572	4,969	9,860	10,331	2,981	−785	3,898	8,011	15,284	7,064	4,273	1,015	70,473

(All figures rounded to nearest pound)

Cash flow forecast 19X7 (II)

	Jan £	Feb £	Mar £	Apr £	May £	Jun £	Jul £	Aug £	Sep £	Oct £	Nov £	Dec £	Total £
Sales receipts	106,154	106,154	171,026	203,167	283,667	318,167	226,167	149,500	195,500	264,500	391,000	318,167	2,733,167
Total receipts	106,154	106,154	171,026	203,167	283,667	318,167	226,167	149,500	195,500	264,500	391,000	318,167	2,733,167
Purchase payments	100,000	100,000	337,861	245,111	316,902	165,658	232,702	153,755	454,227	279,147	364,493	101,047	2,850,902
Revenue payments	6,500	6,500	6,500	6,500	6,500	6,500	6,500	6,500	6,500	6,500	6,500	6,500	78,000
Overdraft interest	0	0	4,100	0	0	8,573	0	0	7,906	0	0	12,948	33,527
VAT	0	0	0	−2,535	0	0	−2,505	0	0	−3,345	0	0	−8,385
Total payments	106,500	106,500	348,461	249,076	323,402	180,731	236,697	160,255	468,633	282,302	370,993	120,494	2,954,044
Net cash flow	−346	−346	−177,435	−45,909	−39,735	137,436	−10,531	−10,755	−273,133	−17,802	20,008	197,672	−220,877
Opening bank balance	−138,000	−138,346	−138,692	−316,127	−362,037	−401,772	−264,336	−274,866	−285,621	−558,754	−576,556	−556,549	
Closing bank balance	−138,346	−138,692	−316,127	−362,037	−401,772	−264,336	−274,866	−285,621	−558,754	−576,556	−556,549	−358,877	

(All figures rounded to nearest pound)

Flow of funds statement 19X7 (II)

Source:	£	Application:	£
Deterioration in bank balance	220,877	Increase in debtors	256,833
Increase in creditors	216,619	Increase in stock	251,136
Net profit (before depreciation)	70,473		
	507,969		507,969

End of year liquid figures

Liabilities:	£	Assets:	£
Bank debit balance	358,877	Trade debtors	486,833
Trade creditors	498,605	Closing stock	508,136
Accrued VAT	−1,985		
Accrued interest	0		

Comments on forecasts (II) The profit budget (II) reveals the same sales, £2.6 million, and gross profit £182,000 (7%), but the net profit has dropped to £70,473 as a result of increased bank charges of £33,527 compared with £10,937 in budget (I). This has occurred due to the bank being 'sourced' to carry out the expansion plan.

Let us examine the cash flow (II). The bank peaks at a staggering £576,556 in October and the year end balances are shown with trade credit held at £500,000 and bank closing at £358,000!

The funds flow statement (II) reveals the limitation of an annualised document — it gives no hint that the bank actually peaked at £576,000 in October.

Let us now suppose that trade credit is held at £500,000 and the company's overhead costs actually double in line with sales, as opposed to remaining static.

Profit budget (III)

	Jan £	Feb £	Mar £	Apr £	May £	Jun £	Jul £	Aug £	Sep £	Oct £	Nov £	Dec £	Total £
Forecast sales	160,000	180,000	260,000	280,000	180,000	120,000	180,000	240,000	360,000	260,000	220,000	160,000	2,600,000
	160,000	180,000	260,000	280,000	180,000	120,000	180,000	240,000	360,000	260,000	220,000	160,000	2,600,000
Less:													
Forecast purchases	162,540	185,060	269,300	288,100	185,200	123,400	185,200	246,800	370,300	263,600	220,400	169,236	2,669,136
Stock change	−13,740	−17,660	−27,500	−27,700	−17,800	−11,800	−17,800	−23,600	−35,500	−21,800	−15,800	−20,436	−251,136
Total direct costs	148,800	167,400	241,800	260,400	167,400	111,600	167,400	223,200	334,800	241,800	204,600	148,800	2,418,000
Gross profit	11,200	12,600	18,200	19,600	12,600	8,400	12,600	16,800	25,200	18,200	15,400	11,200	182,000
Less:													
Revenue payments	13,000	13,000	13,000	13,000	13,000	13,000	13,000	13,000	13,000	13,000	13,000	13,000	156,000
Monthly interest	1,155	1,211	1,973	2,957	3,360	2,979	2,555	2,695	3,875	5,158	5,202	4,313	37,432
Trading profit	−2,955	−1,611	3,227	3,643	−3,760	−7,579	−2,955	1,105	8,325	42	−2,802	−6,113	−11,432

(All figures rounded to nearest pound)

Cash flow forecast 19X7 (III)

	Jan £	Feb £	Mar £	Apr £	May £	Jun £	Jul £	Aug £	Sep £	Oct £	Nov £	Dec £	Total £
Sales receipts	106,154	106,154	171,026	203,167	283,667	318,167	226,167	149,500	195,500	264,500	391,000	318,167	2,733,167
Total receipts	106,154	106,154	171,026	203,167	283,667	318,167	226,167	149,500	195,500	264,500	391,000	318,167	2,733,167
Purchase payments	100,000	100,000	337,861	245,111	316,902	165,658	232,702	153,755	454,227	279,147	364,493	101,047	2,850,902
Revenue payments	13,000	13,000	13,000	13,000	13,000	13,000	13,000	13,000	13,000	13,000	13,000	13,000	156,000
Overdraft interest	0	0	4,339	0	0	9,295	0	0	9,124	0	0	14,673	37,432
VAT	0	0	0	−2,535	0	0	−2,505	0	0	−3,345	0	0	−8,385
Total payments	113,000	113,000	355,200	255,576	329,902	187,953	243,197	166,755	476,351	288,802	377,493	128,720	3,035,948
Net cash flow	−6,846	−6,846	−184,174	−52,409	−46,235	130,214	−17,031	−17,255	−280,851	−24,302	13,508	189,447	−302,782
Opening bank balance	−138,000	−144,846	−151,692	−335,866	−388,276	−434,511	−304,297	−321,328	−338,583	−619,434	−643,736	−630,228	
Closing bank balance	−144,846	−151,692	−335,866	−388,276	−434,511	−304,297	−321,328	−338,583	−619,434	−643,736	−630,228	−440,782	

(All figures rounded to nearest pound)

Flow of funds statement 19X7 (III)

Source:	£	Application:	£
Deterioration in bank balance	302,782	Increase in debtors	256,833
Increase in creditors	216,619	Increase in stock	251,136
		Net loss (before depreciation)	11,432
	519,401		519,401

End of year liquid figures

Liabilities:	£	Assets:	£
Bank debit balance	440,782	Trade debtors	486,833
Trade creditors	498,605	Closing stock	508,136
Accrued VAT	−1,985		
Accrued interest	0		

Comments on forecasts (III) The profit budget (III) again shows sales £2.6 million, gross profit £182,000 (7%), but with overheads doubled at £156,000 we are now showing a *loss* of £11,432.

The cash flow (III) is even worse, with the bank now peaking at £643,736 in October.

The year end closing figures in funds flow statement (III) show trade credit restricted to £500,000 and bank closing at £440,782.

It now looks pretty gloomy! As a final throw, let us suppose trade credit is held at £500,000, overhead costs double, and with the increased sales the gross margin drops by 2% to 5%. Remember that in previous years the gross margin was a falling trend:

	19X4	19X5	19X6	19X7
	10%	9%	7%	?
On a turnover of	£900,000	£1,050,000	£1,300,00	£2,600,000

Profit budget (IV)

	Jan £	Feb £	Mar £	Apr £	May £	Jun £	Jul £	Aug £	Sep £	Oct £	Nov £	Dec £	Total £
Forecast sales	160,000	180,000	260,000	280,000	180,000	120,000	180,000	240,000	360,000	260,000	220,000	160,000	2,600,000
	160,000	180,000	260,000	280,000	180,000	120,000	180,000	240,000	360,000	260,000	220,000	160,000	2,600,000
Less:													
Forecast purchases	165,740	188,660	274,500	293,700	188,800	125,800	188,800	251,600	377,500	268,800	224,800	172,436	2,721,136
Stock change	−13,740	−17,660	−27,500	−27,700	−17,800	−11,800	−17,800	−23,600	−35,500	−21,800	−15,800	−20,436	−251,136
Total direct costs	152,000	171,000	247,000	266,000	171,000	114,000	171,000	228,000	342,000	247,000	209,000	152,000	2,470,000
Gross profit	8,000	9,000	13,000	14,000	9,000	6,000	9,000	12,000	18,000	13,000	11,000	8,000	130,000
Less:													
Revenue payments	13,000	13,000	13,000	13,000	13,000	13,000	13,000	13,000	13,000	13,000	13,000	13,000	156,000
Monthly interest	1,155	1,211	1,994	3,010	3,450	3,108	2,710	2,874	4,102	5,439	5,524	4,673	39,250
Trading profit	−6,155	−5,211	−1,994	−2,010	−7,450	−10,108	−6,710	−3,874	898	−5,439	−7,524	−9,673	−65,250

(All figures rounded to nearest pound)

Cash flow forecast 19X7 (IV)

	Jan £	Feb £	Mar £	Apr £	May £	Jun £	Jul £	Aug £	Sep £	Oct £	Nov £	Dec £	Total £
Sales receipts	106,154	106,154	171,026	203,167	283,667	318,167	226,167	149,500	195,500	264,500	391,000	318,167	2,733,167
Total receipts	106,154	106,154	171,026	203,167	283,667	318,167	226,167	149,500	195,500	264,500	391,000	318,167	2,733,167
Purchase payments	100,000	100,000	342,921	249,864	323,035	168,878	237,226	156,745	463,059	284,575	371,623	103,040	2,900,965
Revenue payments	13,000	13,000	13,000	13,000	13,000	13,000	13,000	13,000	13,000	13,000	13,000	13,000	156,000
Overdraft interest	0	0	4,360	0	0	9,569	0	0	9,686	0	0	15,636	39,250
VAT	0	0	0	−4,335	0	0	−4,245	0	0	−5,685	0	0	−14,265
Total payments	113,000	113,000	360,280	258,529	336,035	191,446	245,981	169,745	485,745	291,890	384,623	131,676	3,081,951
Net cash flow	−6,846	−6,846	−189,255	−55,363	−52,368	126,721	−19,814	−20,245	−290,245	−27,390	6,378	186,491	−348,784
Opening bank balance	−138,000	−144,846	−151,692	−340,947	−396,310	−448,678	−321,957	−341,772	−362,016	−652,262	−679,652	−673,274	
Closing bank balance	−144,846	−151,692	−340,947	−396,310	−448,678	−321,957	−341,772	−362,016	−652,262	−679,652	−673,274	−486,784	

(All figures rounded to nearest pound)

Flow of funds statement 19X7 (IV)

Source:	£	Application:	£
Deterioration in bank balance	348,784	Increase in debtors	256,833
Increase in creditors	224,436	Increase in stock	251,136
		Net loss (before depreciation)	65,250
	573,220		573,220

End of year liquid figures

Liabilities:	£	Assets:	£
Bank debit balance	486,784	Trade debtors	486,833
Trade creditors	508,341	Closing stock	508,136
Accrued VAT	−3,905		
Accrued interest	0		

Comments on forecasts (IV) The profit budget (IV) reveals sales £2.6 million, gross profit down to £130,000 (5%), overheads at £156,000 and a big loss this time of £65,250.

The associated cash flow forecast (IV) reveals the highest peak yet, at £679,652 with the year end closing at £486,784 (funds flow statement (IV)).

Conclusions In the light of all the above forecasts, would *you* back Clothing Imports plans to double turnover? Perhaps a more modest increase would be more prudent? In any event, this case study most certainly illustrated the working capital demands of an expanding business. It is worth remembering that with any plan for business expansion it could be opportune to look at a financial 'package', e.g., factoring, leasing, new capital, etc. (see Chapter 11).

10 Monitoring

When the bank has a debenture charge, then monthly figures (as well as monitoring business performance through ratio analysis, cash flow and management information) can be called for to help monitor the bank advance. After considering the nature of the debenture charge in general we will look at the type of monitoring that can be used.

THE DEBENTURE CHARGE

Bankers will frequently encounter situations where a company customer has executed a debenture charge to the bank. This type of security will give the bank differing priorities over the company assets. Forms of charge vary between banks but a debenture usually gives the bank the following security:

(a) a legal mortgage over all freehold and leasehold property together with buildings fixtures and fixed plant and machinery;

(b) an equitable fixed first charge on after-acquired property including fixed plant and machinery;

(c) a fixed first charge on present book debts and future book debts;

(d) a first floating charge over all the other assets of the company, both present and future.

The debenture usually specifies within the charge form the right to appoint a receiver after demand for payment of money's secured or at the request of the company's directors.

The receiver's powers will generally include the right to:

(a) take possession of and sell off assets;
(b) carry on the business and borrow money on the security of the assets;
(c) appoint managers and agents to assist with running the business;
(d) carry out acts incidental to the performance of his duties.

Limitations of the charge

Any preferential creditors, e.g., VAT, PAYE, will erode available floating charge recoveries. However, a bank can rank in priority with other preferentials in respect of advances for wages and salaries. Under the Insolvency Act 1986, sch. 6, para. 11, money advanced and actually paid to employees during the four months prior to winding-up will be valid subject to a maximum of £800 in respect of each employee.

Furthermore it must be remembered that under s. 245 of the Insolvency Act 1986, floating charges granted within 12 months prior to the commencement of winding-up are invalid unless it can be proved that the company was solvent at the time the charge was created. Usually, however, *Clayton's* case will assist, in that the debt will often have been turned over by receipts and payments through the account, and the advance will be deemed to represent new money. In these cases the floating charge will then be valid.

(See also p.136 on reservation of title to stock.)

SETTING A FORMULA

In setting a formula for cover of the bank debt by current assets, the banker will need to consider both the balance sheet strength and the nature of the risk. For example, for an old-established, successful business having substantial fixed assets a finer margin of cover may be stipulated than for a relatively new, expanding business with few fixed assets.

Furthermore, regard must be given both to the annual accounts and also to the current levels of book debts to make sure that any formula set is workable. A formula could be two and a half times cover of the bank debt by stock and debtors, with cover of one and a half times by book debts.

A further guide to workable formulae is to look at profit/cash budgets (if these documents have been prepared) and derive from them a monthly projected balance sheet.

There are many possible variations of the formula, but whatever the margin of cover decided upon, any breach of the set formula may be used by the banker as a 'trigger' to call for interim financial accounts or call for an independent review of the company's affairs by an accountant.

MONITORING THE FORMULA

To enable effective monitoring of the formula it is advisable to use some kind of debenture monitoring form. A suggested layout is shown in example 1. With such a form the listing of figures for debtors, stock, creditors, etc., from the latest available annual accounts forms a useful base for comparison with current figures on a month to month basis. The bank balance used should be as per the *company's books*. Sales per annum and sales per month have been included. If businesses are carrying out any monitoring at all it is almost certain to be sales! This information will enable you to monitor current sales activity. Capital expenditures or disposals should be minuted — they will have an effect on liquidity movements. The current assets total line A should then be compared with the agreed lending cover formula to ensure compliance.

COMPANY NAME: FINANCIAL YEAR END . . . .

AGREED FORMULA:

	From annual accounts date . . . . . £	From company books: Jan £	Feb £	Mar £	Apr £	May £	Jun £
Current assets Cash Debtors Stock							
Total (A)							
Current liabilities Bank Creditors							
Total (B)							
Net of totals (A-B)							

Capital expenditure (disposals)

Sales record per annum per month

Example 1 Debenture monitoring form

CRITICAL ANALYSIS OF VARIATIONS

As well as monitoring the debenture cover formula of bank debt to current assets, the monitoring form is also useful in highlighting the net current asset movement position (net of totals: A – B), as the following example shows.

ABC Co.

The figures shown overleaf are applicable to this company.

For ABC Co:

(a) The formula was 2½ times cover by debtors and stock — this was easily maintained each month.

(b) The net current assets position (A – B) shows an improving trend from January to May but suddenly drops back in June. (Why did this occur?)

However, comparing the June end position with the opening figures shows an improvement of £47,825 (£346,795 – £298,970). Although this does not always represent a profit figure, it does show as a *healthy* sign — this positive movement can only be caused by profits earned or funds injected or sale of fixed assets or a combination of all three.

Equally, if the movement was negative (as occurred from May to June), further enquiry would be justified.

(c) The annual sales of £2.4 million average out to £200,000 per month. Monthly sales recorded on the form look good in comparison, and it will be interesting to see the full 12 months picture.

The next example illustrates the *difficulties* which can be encountered with debenture monitoring figures.

R Co.

R Co. is engaged in manufacturing and was established in 19X3. Sales have progressed and the bank account reveals the following statistics:

Year ended	Average balance	Turnover
	£	£
19X3	5,818 Cr	1,600,000
19X4	79,663 Dr	2,600,000
19X5	124,212 Dr	3,100,000
19X6	50,003 Dr	3,000,000
(to date: August 19X6)		

COMPANY NAME: ABC

FINANCIAL YEAR END 31 December

AGREED FORMULA: 2½ times debtors plus stock

	From annual accounts date 31.12.X5 £	From company books:					
		Jan £	Feb £	Mar £	Apr £	May £	Jun £
Current assets							
Cash	2,500	1,800	2,600	1,500	2,800	3,200	1,800
Debtors	484,500	472,653	486,152	517,250	586,220	570,185	526,590
Stock	120,000	135,500	140,200	120,700	115,800	112,100	110,500
Total (A)	607,000	609,953	628,952	639,450	704,820	685,485	638,890
Current liabilities							
Bank	115,850	108,950	120,680	105,700	102,800	100,849	98,774
Creditors	192,180	210,525	200,520	225,600	210,723	202,576	197,821
Total (B)	308,030	319,475	321,200	331,300	313,523	303,425	296,595
Net of totals (A-B)	298,970	290,478	307,752	308,150	391,297	382,060	346,795
Capital expenditure — Nil	PER ANNUM	PER MONTH					
		Jan	Feb	Mar	Apr	May	Jun
Sales record	2.4 m	215,280	325,650	350,320	325,000	328,520	255,650

19X6 analysis:
Best balance £77,454 Cr
Worst balance £185,917 Dr

Overdraft limit: £200,000
Security: debenture
Formula: 2½ times current assets

A summary of the annual accounts for 19X4 and 19X5 illustrates profitable trading and retentions:

Year ended:	December 19X5	December 19X4
Sales	£2,900,000	£2,400,000
Gross profit %	31%	34%
Profit	£136,000	£190,000
Net worth	£367,000	£256,000

Note that whilst turnover has increased, it has been at the expense of the gross margin. However, everything looks straightforward until the debenture monitoring figures held at the branch are reviewed. An extract of the net liquid position appears overleaf.

The debenture formula has been easily met (bank × 2½ : current assets) but what has happened to the liquid surplus totals (A – B)? The surplus has fallen from £927,000 in January to £844,000 in June.

Further review will show that the stock figure looks 'silly'. It cannot be static for three consecutive months in a manufacturing business!

Interim management accounts are called for and they show:

To June 19X6:	
Sales	£2,600,000
Gross profit	30%
Net profit	£116,000

Certainly a much healthier position than revealed in the debenture montioring figures! The problem was of course the stock figure — not even estimated — it was only a repeat of the previous quarter-end figure. The 'true' stock figure, when verified, was almost £200,000 more.

ADDITIONAL ANALYSIS

You will have seen how important it is to understand *fully* the figures presented on the debenture monitoring form. For this reason it is suggested that the following additional analyses are made, by way of supplementary forms attached to the debenture monitoring form.

COMPANY NAME: R

FINANCIAL YEAR END 31 December

AGREED FORMULA: 2½ times cover

	From annual accounts date 31.12.X5 £000	From company books:					
		Jan £000	Feb £000	Mar £000	Apr £000	May £000	Jun £000
Current assets							
Debtors	811	822	928	929	1,014	1,059	1,045
Stock	673	693	693	663	663	663	663
Total (A)	1,484	1,515	1,621	1,622	1,677	1,722	1,708
Current liabilities							
Bank	107	107	109	75	126	240	165
Creditors	380	425	443	514	612	634	664
Hire-purchase	65	56	66	71	30	23	35
Total (B)	552	588	618	660	768	897	864
Net of totals (A-B)	932	927	1,003	962	909	825	844

Debtors

This figure needs breaking down into normal trade, inter-company, and doubtful debt. Care should be taken not to include any debts which have been factored under a factoring agreement. Further, it is useful to get an indication of debtor spread and debtor control. See examples 2 and 3.

DEBTOR	TOTALS	AGE (days)				REMARKS
		Current	30	60	90	
£1,000 and over Others						
PERCENTAGES	100%	%	%	%	%	

Example 2 Debtor analysis

NAME	Total balance	Current	30 days	60 days	90 days	REMARKS
Totals						

Example 3 Debtor analysis by major customer account

Stock

This figure is a difficult one for many businesses to provide. Frequently there will be many differing stock-lines and the only accurate way is to carry out a physical stock-check. However, this difficulty can be overcome if the stock-file is computerised. Usually, though, in practice you will have to accept the directors' estimate based on stock movements during the month. A quarterly *physical* stock-take should be encouraged to give a clear indicator of the *actual* stock position — useful to both the banker and the customer!

A further complication is in businesses where there is on-going product manufacture or job contracts — then it will be necessary to estimate work-in-progress.

Also stock can be invoiced from a supplier subject to reservation of title (*Romalpa* terms). This reservation means that goods supplied remain the property of the supplier *until he is paid*. Again the directors should provide details. Example 4 illustrates stock analysis.

Month ended		
Stock	£	as a %
Raw materials Work in progress Finished goods Total stock*		
*Reservation of title £.		

Example 4 Analysis of manufacturing stock

It is useful, when stock is physically taken and valued, to mark the stock figure on the debenture monitoring form accordingly.

Creditors

In addition to age analysis (example 5) to see if there is pressure for payment on the business, it is also very useful to split the creditors total into normal trade and preferential (example 6). We are very interested in the preferential creditors for the reasons stated at the beginning of this chapter when we considered the debenture charge.

We should establish if there are any set-off trading positions between creditors and debtors which might lead to counter-claims.

CREDITOR	TOTALS	AGE				REMARKS
		Current	30 days	60 days	90 days	
£1,000 and over Others						
PERCENTAGES	100%	%	%	%	%	

Example 5 Creditor analysis

CREDITOR	TOTALS	Age				REMARKS
		Current	30 days	60 days	90 days	
Trade: Preferential creditors VAT PAYE/NIC etc.						
TOTALS						

Example 6 Creditor analysis by major customer account

PROTECTING THE BANK'S POSITION

It is always difficult to advise on timing of the appointment of a receiver and manager. Sometimes the company directors will request it; but often it is a case of the company directors hoping for better times and wanting to carry on — while the bank is anxiously looking at the trading of the business and pressure on the bank account.

How best can you protect the bank's position? If it is a hopeless case, then you must act decisively. Delay may cause further deterioration.

If all parties are slightly unsure of their ground, then a useful interim step is to get the company to agree to the appointment of an investigating accountant. His brief will vary but essentially it is to:

(a) comment on and analyse recent trading;
(b) draw up a current statement of affairs;
(c) comment on the future viability of the business;
(d) comment on the bank's exposure and security.

The appointee should be an accountant with proven expertise, with knowledge of the particular trade (if possible), and if receivership follows you must feel sure that he will be the man for the job.

The investigation can be quick and it may only take from three to five days to get a 'feel' for the business and make a preliminary report. The company directors *should* cooperate, as it must be also in *their* interest to know where they stand.

The following case study will illustrate the speed with which the bank's position can deteriorate.

CASE STUDY: M GROUP LTD

This group was involved in cash and carry wines and spirits with three warehouses and six retail shops. The business commenced in 1960 and had grown rapidly in recent years. The board of four directors included the proprietor and his wife, a sales director and a chartered accountant acting as finance director.

You have been unable to obtain recent debenture figures due to the company transferring records to computer. There has been pressure of late on the bank account and you have had to report temporary excess positions to the control department. The company directors have told you that the bank account problem is only temporary and is mainly caused by the cost of a move of premises.

However, draft accounts have just been produced to the company year-end 31 March, and when you compare them with previous years, the following is revealed:

	Draft accounts 31.3.X6	19X5	Audited accounts 19X4	19X3
Sales	£36.1 m	£30.4 m	£19 m	£9.3 m
Gross profit	£1.2 m	£1.3 m	£909,000	£586,000
Gross profit %	3.4 %	4.2 %	4.8 %	6.2 %
Overheads	£1.7 m	£1.1 m	£689,000	£485,000
Profit (Loss)	(£484,000)	£147,000	£220,000	£101,000

The group results indicate the rapid growth of the business in the last four years, with sales going from £9.3 million to £36.1 million, and with a fine (and deteriorating) gross margin, down from 6.2 % to 3.4 %.

The draft accounts reveal both a drop in gross margin and at the same time increased overheads, to £1.7 million, resulting in a loss of £484,000.

With the move of premises and transfer to computer, no management accounts were prepared during the latter part of the year to 31.3.X6, and consequently the considerable loss came as a shock to the directors.

The directors agreed to the appointment of investigating accounts to try to pinpoint the current trading position and cash flow requirement. The accountants subsequently reported:

(a) a serious inbalance of trade between volume of sales, gross margins and overheads incurred;

(b) that the accounting records maintained were *most inadequate* for a business of this nature with fine gross margins and high volume of turnover.

The following figures were provided to illustrate the bank's position:

		At 31.3.X6		At 20.5.X6	
		Draft balance sheet	Estimated break-up balance sheet	Estimated balance sheet	Estimated break-up balance sheet
Assets subject to fixed charge:		£000	£000	£000	£000
Freehold deeds		283	175	283	175
Leasehold		9	—	9	—
Goodwill		70	—	70	—
Trade debtors		1,318	1,197	1,102	956
	(A)	1,680	1,372	1,464	1,131
Assets subject to floating charge:					
Fixtures & equipment		420	50	420	50
Motor vehicles		60	30	60	30
Stock		5,568	4,202	4,150	3,058
		6,048	4,282	4,630	3,138
Less: Preferential creditors:					
PAYE/NIC		(28)	(28)	(58)	(58)
VAT		(299)	(299)	(799)	(799)
Wages & holiday pay		(10)	(23)	(10)	(23)
Other preferentials		(3)	(3)	(66)	(66)
		(340)	(353)	(933)	(946)
Net floating charge (B) assets		5,708	3,929	3,697	2,192
Total realisable (A + B)		7,388	5,301	5,161	3,323
Bank		2,510	2,510	2,743	2,743
Surplus on bank's (C) charge		4,878	2,791	2,418	580
Unsecured creditors		4,459	3,759	1,999	1,399
Net assets/(liabilities)		419	(968)	419	(819)

The accountants also made the following report:

> The group business has such a high turnover of stocks with very short periods of credit given and taken that the balance sheet can change dramatically in short periods of time — this is highlighted by the reduction of surplus on the bank's charge on a going concern basis between 31/3 and 20/5 from £4.8 million to £2.4 million.
>
> [See also break-up basis, £2.8 million to £580,000: line (c).]
>
> In our view the bank's position is not satisfactory . . . the bank can never be sure as to what the position is . . .
>
> Losses are highly likely to be continuing . . .

A few weeks later a receiver was appointed.

DEBENTURE REALISATIONS: BREAK-UP VALUES

What you recover as a percentage of book debts, stock or fixed assets varies enormously from trade to trade and area to area. The recoveries unit in the bank's regional office will be able to give you a guide based on their experiences. *Full* recovery on each asset is rare — that is why we set a formula for cover in the first place, which we hope will provide an overall *margin* at the end of the day.

Here is an interesting case study to show you what *can* happen.

CASE STUDY: COMPANY X

Company X were UK distributors for domestic kitchen appliances. Sales were mainly to electrical wholesalers and kitchen specialists. The goods carried *no* manufacturer's guarantee but were distributed by Company X with their own 12 months' warranty.

Company X traded profitably in its early years but later incurred substantial losses due to abortive ventures into new kitchen and bathroom products. At the same time high warranty charges were encountered with one major product line and business overheads also increased during 19X1 and 19X2:

Year ended December:	19W9	19X0	19X1	19X2
Sales	£2.57 m	£3.56 m	£4.23 m	£2.3 m
Gross profit %	19%	18%	18%	17%
Overheads	£493,000	£641,000	£965,000	£783,000
Overheads/sales %	19%	18%	23%	34%
Net profit/(loss)	—	—	(£202,000)	(£323,000)

Investigating accountants went in in September 19X3 (after the bank received the disastrous 19X2 trading figures) and reported that the bank debt *should* be covered on a break-up basis:

Estimated statement of affairs as at 30.9.X3

	Book value	Break-up value
Assets subject to fixed charge:	£000	£000
Debtors	425	335
Less: Bank	(393)	(393)
Surplus/(shortfall) to debenture holder under fixed charge	32	(58)
Assets subject to floating charge:		
Stock	497	251
Plant/machinery/motor vehicles	33	15
	530	266

		Book value £000	Break-up value £000
Preferential creditors:			
PAYE/NI	36		
Rates	12		
VAT	130		
Employees (holiday pay)	3	(181)	(181)
Surplus available under floating charge		349	85
Surplus/(shortfall) to debenture holder		32	(58)
		381	27
Unsecured creditors		(553)	(553)
Shortfall to unsecured creditors		(172)	(526)

(You will see that most of the bank's cover was on book debts as a fixed charge.)

When receivership took place later in December 19X3 the bank's cover on debtors was quickly dissipated with many counter-claims from customers to set-off on warranty work and also retentions in case of *future* complaints on warranty work.

Finally, by 19X6 the total recovery from book debts amounted to only £134,000 as against the initial book value of £425,000.

Stock also suffered, although previously discounted by 50% to £251,000. Eventual realisation was only £125,000 (50% of the discounted figure).

CONCLUSION

To put this chapter into perspective, it must be stated that there will be many debenture lendings where there will be no problems. There will also be cases where the debenture formula is easily met due to expanding sales leading to increasing book debts; recall our case study on Clothing Imports — the business' liquidity must then be considered.

From the banker's point of view the on-going expanding business can cause a dilemma. The rapid growth in the turnover and consequent additional borrowing requirement can cause an adverse capital gearing situation (bank limit : net worth) unless there are profit retentions. Hence an additional retention formula could be considered and it would be wise to call for supporting management accounts to illustrate on-going profitability.

A final reminder — in analysing business performance we need to review:

* bank account trends
* if SBLGS, product documentation
* balance sheets and trading accounts

* funds flow statements
* management accounts
* projections
* debenture monitoring

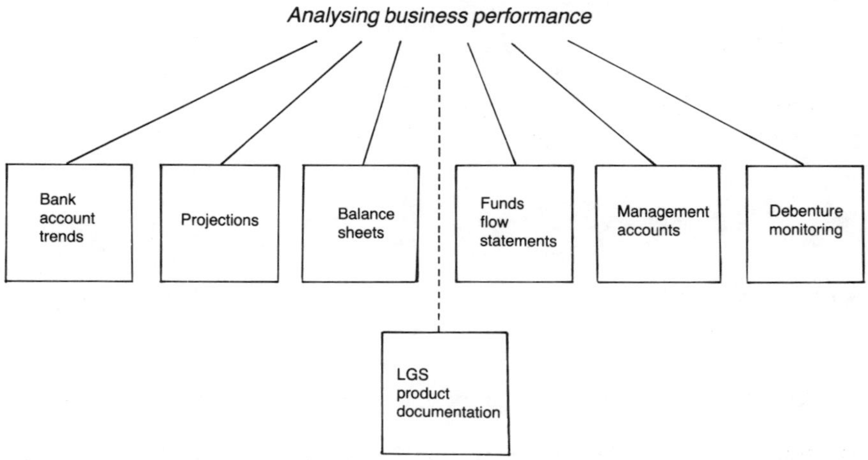

At the beginning of Part Two we stated that the five basic points to be considered were:

(a) How much is required?
(b) What is to be done with the money?
(c) What are the plans for repayment?
(d) What will be the bank's position if the plans for repayment go wrong?
(e) What is the experience and track record of the borrower?

I hope that you will now be able to deal more confidently with these points.

Part Three

Financial support for businesses

11 Finance available through the banks

Virtually all small firms operate an account with one of the clearing banks; as a result the banks are the main — and in many cases the only — point of contact that small firms have with the financial system. In the past few years, the banks have developed a large number of schemes and facilities to supplement their traditional services for small firms. They now have a wide range to offer to the small business customer. In some cases different banks have chosen to pursue different paths — individual banks have launched particularly distinctive services. The bank's services have attracted considerable interest and have helped to demonstrate responsiveness to the financial needs of their business customers. The major part of the bank's support for small firms continues to take the form of overdrafts and loans, managerial advice and other traditional banking services.

OVERDRAFTS AND LOANS

The clearing bank overdraft remains the most versatile form of finance available to the business customer. Within limits, the amount borrowed can fluctuate in response to the flow of cash passing through the customer's account. Interest is charged on each day's outstanding balance. The overdraft is cheaper than any other form of external finance (depending on the taxation situation).

Overdrafts are intended to cover short-term borrowing, to finance stock and work in progress. The sale of the finished product will generate the funds for repaying the borrowing. However, an increasing proportion of overdraft lending has taken on a 'hard core' quality and many firms operate their accounts permanently with an overdrawn balance.

Some 'hard core' overdrafts have been used to finance plant and machinery. Nevertheless, it is generally regarded as more prudent for longer-term assets to be financed by longer-term funds, rather than by overdraft which have a variable rate of interest and which are technically repayable on demand. The result has been the growth of term lending in the past few years. About half the bank's lending now takes the form of term loans repayable over periods ranging from a year to as many as 20 years. These loans can be tailored to the circumstances of the borrowers. Term loans are particularly suitable for financing investments in new assets, where the repayment schedule can be related to the cash flow. They have an increasing relevance for firms with plans for expansion.

VENTURE CAPITAL

The equity capital of a business is the owner's capital permanently invested, together with any undistributed profits. Most businesses begin with an individual providing equity capital from his own resources. In recent years the banks have become more directly involved in equity financing by launching special schemes to help meet the equity needs of their small business customers. These investments are generally through subsidiary companies.

In addition to providing venture capital to the new enterprise and development capital to the established, expanding enterprise, the banks may also acquire shares. The banks can help to ensure that control of a family firm remains within the family, by providing a mixture of loan and equity finance. The following section is a guide to development and venture capital facilities.

Sources of venture capital

Vehicle for capital	*Backers*	*Type of client or situation*	*Min/Max funds injected*	*Start-up capital*	*Equity stake*	*Term of funding*
Abingworth Tel: (01) 839 6745	Leading UK and European institutions	Usually established profitable companies	£100,000-£500,000 and occasionally larger amounts	Possibly, if management of proven calibre	Always minority	Open
Advent Eurofund Ltd Tel: Jersey (0534) 75151	Monsanto: 50% UK financial institutions, universities and colleges: 50%	New technology at all stages of development	£100,000 to £500,000	Yes, but not exclusively	Significant minority	Flexible
Anglo-American Venture Fund Ltd Tel: (061) 236 7302	British Technology Group (BTG)	New technology, with emphasis on electronics	Up to £300,000 but will syndicate	Yes	Yes	Equity and preference shares
APA Venture Capital Fund Tel: (01) 388 1811	Pension funds, insurance companies and institutions primarily from the UK	Companies with high growth prospects, management buy-outs	£100,000-£1m	Yes	Minority equity investments	Approx 5 years
Barclays Development Capital Tel: (01) 623 4321	Barclays Bank Group	Established growth companies earning £100,000+ pre-tax	£150,000 min but may syndicate large investments	No	Yes, 10-40%	Open

Finance available through the banks

Vehicle for capital	*Backers*	*Type of client or situation*	*Min/Max funds injected*	*Start-up capital*	*Equity stake*	*Term of funding*
Biotechnology Investments Ltd Tel: (01) 280 5000	NM Rothschild and leading UK institutions	Biotechnology companies worldwide at all stages of development	Flexible: generally \$500,000-\$2m; would syndicate larger investments	Yes	Up to 20%, exceptionally higher	Flexible; usually equity
Birmingham Technology Ltd Tel: (021) 359 0981	Lloyds Bank plc; Birmingham City Council; University of Aston in Birmingham	Hi-tech research, development and/or hi-tech manufacturing companies	Depending on requirements	Yes	Possibly, but not exclusively	Flexible according to requirements
Brown Shipley Developments Tel: (01) 606 9833	Brown, Shipley & Co.	Quality of individuals of prime importance and above average growth sectors	£50,000 min equity preference shares, may syndicate larger investments and loans	Yes, if individuals have previous experience	Yes, usually 10-30%	Equity: open Loans: up to 8 years
Candover Investments Tel: (01) 583 5090	7 leading UK institutions	Management buy-outs and conventional development capital situations	£2 m +	No	Always minority	Open
Citicorp Development Capital Tel: (01) 438 1280	Citicorp/ Citibank	Expansion capital for technology growth companies. Management buy-outs Acquisition etc, finance for mature companies	£200,000-£5 m	Exceptionally; proven management team and high growth prospects required	Yes 10-40% desired	Open, structured to suit company requirement
Clydesdale Bank Industrial Finance Tel: (041) 248 7070	Clydesdale Bank/ Midland Bank	Profitable private companies with potential for growth	Normally £100,000+ but will consider proposals at lower level	Yes—highly selective	Normally 20-40%	Open
Commercial Bank of the Near East Tel: (01) 283 4041	Range of shareholders predominant Greek	Small and medium sized companies, public & private	Up to £400,000	Yes	No	Open

Vehicle for capital	*Backers*	*Type of client or situation*	*Min/Max funds injected*	*Start-up capital*	*Equity stake*	*Term of funding*
Common-wealth Development Finance Company Ltd Tel: (01) 407 9711	Several common-wealth central banks and 140 major UK companies	Company with proven management and profit record preferably seeking funds for expansion	£300,000 to £1.5 m	No	Yes, 10-45%	Up to 10 years
Council for Small Industries in Rural areas (CoSIRA) Tel: Salisbury (0722) 6255	HM Government plus financial institutions including ICF under new scheme	Companies with no more than 20 skilled employees in countryside or in towns with less than 10,000 population	£250-£75,000 or max ⅓ or ½ of project cost, depending upon location	Loans are available for new starters	No	Building loans: 20 years working capital, equipment loans: 5 years
County Bank Tel: (01) 638 6000	National Westminster Bank	Any growing company with proven management; finance for the company, to enable shareholders to realise part of their investment or to assist management in buying an equity stake	£100,000+	Yes for sound projects	If appropriate often 10-15% usually less than 25%	Loans up to 20 years; equity open
Development Capital Group Tel: (01) 486 5021	Insurance and pension funds, industrial companies and a major clearing bank	Proven management. Minimum £100,000 pre-tax profit potential	£150,000-£1.5m+	Yes, under certain circumstances	Yes, minority	5 years upwards
East of Scotland Industrial Investments Tel: Edinburgh (031) 225 7515	Leading UK institutions	Established profitable companies	£20,000-£400,000	Occasionally, if proven management	Always minority	Equity and long-term loan capital
East of Scotland Onshore Tel: (031) 225 7515	Leading UK institutions	Established companies — the oil service sector	£30,000-£1m	Occasionally, if proven management	Yes, always minority	Equity and long-term capital
EDITH plc Tel: (01) 928 7822	Listed authorised investment trust, (managed by ICFC)	Estblished private and unlisted public companies and smaller listed companies	£5,000-£1m	No	Yes, minority, enabling shareholders to realise investment	Provision of cash or exchange of shares for personal shareholders of family trusts

Finance available through the banks

Vehicle for capital	*Backers*	*Type of client or situation*	*Min/Max funds injected*	*Start-up capital*	*Equity stake*	*Term of funding*
Electra Risk Capital Tel: (01) 836 7766	Private individual investors	Investment qualifying for business start-up relief. Start-ups and companies who have traded for less than 5 years	£100,000 to £750,000 over a period	Yes	Yes to 50%	Only equity investment — no dividend
English & Caledonian plc Tel: (01) 626 7197 (01) 283 3531	Clients of Gartmore Investment, Scottish United Investors and other investors	Private companies able and willing to obtain a USM placing or a full listing within 5 years	£200,000-£750,000 Larger sund can be syndicated among existing shareholders	Yes, if management has previous experience in similar markets	Yes 10-49%	Preferably an equity stake. Loans can be arranged subject to an equity stake
Equity Capital for Industry Tel: (01) 606 8513	City industrial institutions	£200,000-£2m companies with capitalisation of £1m-£40m or similar unquoted	Exceptionally smaller sums available from associate fund	Yes, usually	Long-term: 5-25%	Equity/ convertible/ loan package tailored to circumstances
European Investment Bank (European Community's long-term bank) Tel: (01) 839 3351	(1) Scheme operated by Dol and Scottish, Welsh and Northern Ireland Offices (2) Schemes operated by ICFC, Midland Bank (3) Schemes operated by WDA, SDA and Clydesdale Bank (4) Scheme operated by ICFC (under Orto facility)	For small and medium sized ventures (in UK assisted areas for (1), (2) and (3))	In all cases max contribution is 50% of fixed asset cost of project (1) Loans between 15,000 and £4.15m (2) £15,000 and £2m (3) £15,000 and £250,000 (4) £15,000-£250,000	Loans can be made for sound projects by new companies with adequate equity	No	(1) 7 years including 2-year capital repayment moratorium. Variable rate in region of 9% (2), (3) and (4). Up to 8 years including 2-year capital repayment moratorium. Fixed rate in region of 10%
Federation Pension Fund Tel: (01) 636 3828	The National Federation of Self-Employed and Small Businesses, City of Westminster Assurance	Established self-employed/small business; 3-year record; must be a member of the Federation	£15,000-£250,000 now under review	No	No	Up to 20 years

Vehicle for capital	*Backers*	*Type of client or situation*	*Min/Max funds injected*	*Start-up capital*	*Equity stake*	*Term of funding*
First Welsh General Investment Trust Ltd Tel: (0222) 396131	Commercial Bank of Wales plc	Management buy-out	Subject to negotiation	In certain circumstances	Yes and/or option — not essential	Up to 10 years
Fountain Development Capital Fund Tel: (01) 628 8011	Hill Samuel, pension funds and insurance companies	Any company with 2 years' trading record	£50,000-£750,000	Yes, in certain situations	Always minority	Equity and/or loan
Gresham Trust Tel: (01) 606 6474	Grovewood Securities Ltd (Ultimate holding company Eagle Star Holdings plc)	Profitable private companies looking for expansion, realisation of shareholder's interests, help in management buy-outs	£50,000-£500,000 Will syndicate larger amounts	Where experience and track record exists in previous business	Usually, but always a minority holding	Preference shares or loans: 5-10 years Equity: open
Guidehouse Ltd Tel: (01) 606 6321	Private	Completely open and flexible. Syndicated purchases, management buy-outs, USM venture or development capital	Up to £200,000 directly — syndicate or advise in larger situations	Yes	Preferably yes, but flexible approach, e.g., royalty income	Open and flexible
Hafren Investment Finance Ltd Tel: (044 385) 2666	Welsh Development Agency	High growth operations	£10,000-£100,000	Yes	Yes	Open
Hambro International Venture Fund Tel: (01) 588 2851	Various	Growth companies	$250,000-$500,000	Yes	Yes	Variable
Hambros Advanced Technology Trust Tel: (01) 242 9900	Hambros Bank	Technology industries, high-growth	£100,000-£500,000	Yes	Yes	5 years typical

Finance available through the banks

Vehicle for capital	*Backers*	*Type of client or situation*	*Min/Max funds injected*	*Start-up capital*	*Equity stake*	*Term of funding*
Highlands and Islands Development Board Tel: Inverness (0463) 34171	HM Government (Scottish Office)	Manufacturing, tourist, agriculture, fisheries and other industries in the Scottish Highlands and Islands	Up to £400,000	Yes	Up to 40%	5-10 years. 20 years for building loans
Industrial and Commercial Finance Corporation (ICFC) Tel: (01) 928 7822	Finance for Industry (Bank of England and clearing banks)	Small and medium sized companies public and private	£5,000-£2m	Yes	Yes, minority	Fixed interest loans, medium and long-term
Innotech Investments Limited Tel: (01) 834 2492	Private individuals	Fast growing small to medium sized companies operating in higher technology areas	£100,000 to £500,000	Exceptionally	Yes — minority (25 to 40%)	Equity: open Loans: 3-6 years
INTEX Executives (UK) Ltd and E. P Woods Investments Ltd Tel: (01) 831 6925/ 242 2263	Private and institutional investors and trusts	Industrial and commercial enterprises, with special reference to high technology and innovation	$10,000 to $1m	Yes	Usually minority only. In appropriate circumstances up to 75%	Equity and loan arranged according to circumstances
Larpent Newton & Co. Ltd Tel: (01) 831 9991	Advisory work for leading UK institutions	Unquoted companies requiring development capital and management buy-outs	£50,000-£2m	Yes with experienced management	Usually	Individually tailored
LEDU — The small Business Agency for Northern Ireland Tel: (0232) 691031	Department of Economic Development	Mainly manufacturing and service companies employing up to 50 people in Northern Ireland	£1,500+	Loans, guarantees and grants available	Yes	Grants/ loans/ guarantees average 5 years
London Enterprise Agency Tel: (01) 236 2676	Borough Councils	Encourage growth of small businesses	—	—	—	—

Vehicle for capital	*Backers*	*Type of client or situation*	*Min/Max funds injected*	*Start-up capital*	*Equity stake*	*Term of funding*
Leopold Joseph & Sons Ltd Tel: (01) 588 2323	Leopold Joseph & Sons Ltd and clients	Good management track record, companies with growth record pre-tax profits in excess of £100,000	Open	Exceptionally where entrepreneurs have previous experience and can make a sound financial contribution	Yes	Open
Lovat Enterprise Fund Tel: (01) 621 1212	NCB Pension Funds, Legal & General, Prudential, Electra Investment Trust, Equitable Life	Expansion financing, mainly private companies earning £10,000+ pre-tax	£100,000-£1m	No	5-40%	Open
Mathercourt Securities Ltd Tel: (01) 831 9001	Private and institutional investors	Private UK companies including USM candidates. Close working relationship with management	£25,000-£3.5m syndicatees as appropriate	Yes	Yes, 3-30%	Tailored to suit circum-stances
Melville Street Investments Tel: (031) 226 4071	The British Linen Bank, The Airways Pension Scheme, The Standard Life Assurance Company, Scottish American Investment Company, Scottish Northern Investment Trust, The Edinburgh Investment Trust	Profitable companies with good financial discipline and new companies with established management	£50,000-£500,000 May syndicate larger investments	Yes	Minority capital	Long-term
Meritor Investments Tel: (01) 606 2179	Midland Bank, Rolls Royce Pension Fund	Development situations and shareholders' needs	£100,000-£250,000 May syndicate larger investments	No	Yes, minority	Open
Merseyside Enterprise Fund Ltd Tel: (051) 227 1366	British Technology Group (BTG)	Start-ups and small companies with growth potential	Up to £100,000, syndicate larger investments	Yes	Yes	Open

Finance available through the banks

Vehicle for capital	Backers	Type of client or situation	Min/Max funds injected	Start-up capital	Equity stake	Term of funding
Midland Bank Industrial Equity Holdings Group Tel: (01) 638 8861	Midland Bank	Development situations and shareholders needs	£5,000-£2m	Yes	Yes, minority	Open
Minster Trust Tel: (01) 623 1050	Minster Assets	Small and medium sized companies, public and private companies looking for expansion realisation of shareholders' interests, help for management for buying equity	£100,000-£250,000	Exceptionally, where entrepreneurs have previous experience	Yes, minority	Open
Montagu Investment Management Ltd Tel: (01) 588 1750	Quoted Investment Trusts	Small and medium sized companies public or private, with growth	Normally £200,000 to £3m	Only occasionally	Yes, minority	Open
Moracrest Investments Tel: (01) 628 8409	Midland Bank, Prudential Group and British Gas Pension Fund	Development situations and shareholders' needs	£200,000+ May syndicate larger investments	Yes	Yes, minority	Open
National Westminster Bank under the terms of Capital Loan Scheme (Approach through local branch but if guidance is needed to identify a suitable branch: Tel: (01) 726 1891)		Companies engaged in or planning to set up a business with good growth prospects backed by sound management; must bank or be willing to bank with National Westminster Bank	£10,000-£100,000	Yes	An option to subscribe for shares is taken by a subsidiary, Growth Options Ltd, usually for less than 25% always for less than 50%	Up to 10 years
Newmarket Co. (1981) Ltd (UK subsidiary *Newmarket (Venture (Capital) Ltd)* Tel: (01) 638 4551	London listed company with institutional and general public shareholders	Application of new technology or innovation	Normally US $200,000-$1m but occasionally higher	Yes, but not exclusively	Never a controlling stake	Primarily equity; no requirement for immediate income

Vehicle for capital	*Backers*	*Type of client or situation*	*Min/Max funds injected*	*Start-up capital*	*Equity stake*	*Term of funding*
Noble Grossart Investments Tel: (031) 226 7011	Noble Grossart and Scottish institutional shareholders	Good management in growth 'buy-out' or turnround situations	£50,000-£1m	Yes, if the management has good track record in previous business	Yes, usually 20-40%	Open
Northern Venture Capital Syndicate Tel: (031) 557 3560	Private individuals under the Business Start-Up Scheme	Investments qualifying for Business Start-up Scheme, i.e., start-ups and companies trading for less than 5 years	£25,000 to £75,000	Yes	Yes—up to 50%	Equity capital. Dividends not a priority
Oakland Management Holdings Ltd Tel: Hungerford Berks (04886) 3555	A leading UK institution	New technology growth opportunities	£50,000-£250,000	Not normally	Yes	Flexible up to 7 years
Oakwood Loan Finance Ltd Tel: (01) 403 6666	British Technology Group (BTG)	Small companies with growth potential	£15,000-£50,000	Yes	10% to 20% by option	Option linked, unsecured, 5-year loan. 3-year capital repayment holiday
PA Developments Ltd Tel: (01) 589 7050	Merchant Navy Officers' Pension Fund	Profitable private companies requiring capital for expansion or purchase of existing equity packages stakes. Particularly service industries or technology-based companies	£200,000-to £1m	No	Yes, up to 40%	Equity preferably but will consider equity/loan
Pegasus Holdings Ltd (previously known as Lloyd's Development Capital) Tel: (01) 248 4275	LLoyds Bank Group	Management buy-out, development capital, replacement capital. For companies with proven management, pre-tax profits in excess of £50,000, and with growth potential	Min £100,000. No max, but may syndicate large investments	No	Yes. Usually 10-33⅔%	Flexible

Finance available through the banks

Vehicle for capital	*Backers*	*Type of client or situation*	*Min/Max funds injected*	*Start-up capital*	*Equity stake*	*Term of funding*
Prudential Assurance Company Ltd Tel: (01) 405 9222	Prudential Group	Primarily development capital situations and buy-outs	Typically £50,000-£1m	Ocasionally	Yes	Open
Prutec Tel: (01) 828 2082	Member of the Prudential Group	Development of high technology	Open	Yes	up to 49%	Open
Rainford Venture Capital Tel: St. Helens (0744) 37227	Pilkington Prudential, St. Helens Trust and others	Entrepreneurs; start-up or rapid growth in north west	£50,000-£350,000	Yes	Yes, but preferably not control	Primarily equity. Loans where appropriate to agreed terms
Safeguard Industrial Investments Tel: (01) 581 4455	Over 84% shares held by 17 major insurance companies or pension funds	Small or medium sized UK companies	£50,000-£250,000	Exceptional	Yes	Medium to long
Scottish Allied Investors Tel: Glasgow (041) 204 1321 (041) 226 3551	James Finlay, Royal Bank Development Ltd, Scottish Western Trust Co. Ltd	Profitable private companies looking for expansion capital	£50,000-£500,000	No	Yes, between 20-49%	Medium or long-term investment in equity or loan/equity package
Scottish Development Agency Tel: (041) 248 2700 *Small Business Division* Tel: (031) 343 1911	UK Government	Manufacturing and service businesses operating in Scotland	Open	Yes	Where appropriate	2-20 years equity open
Scottish Offshore Investors Tel: Glasgow (041) 204 1321	James Finlay and other financial institutions	Energy related service companies with growth prospects	£50,000-£250,000	Exceptionally	Yes, between 20-49%	Medium or long-term. Equity or loan/equity
Second Northern Venture Capital Syndicate Tel: (031) 557 3560	Private individuals under the Business Start-up Scheme	Investment qualifying for Business Start-up Scheme, i.e., start-ups and companies trading for less than 5 years	£25,000 min	Yes	Yes—up to 50%	Equity capital dividends not a priority

Vehicle for capital	*Backers*	*Type of client or situation*	*Min/Max funds injected*	*Start-up capital*	*Equity stake*	*Term of funding*
Sharp Unquoted Midland Investment Tel: (021) 236 5801	Legal & General, Royal Insurance Sun Life Assurance Society and others	Successful private companies and management buy-outs	£150,000-£850,000	No	10-35%	Open
Small Company Innovation Fund (SCIF) Tel: (01) 403 6666	British Technology Group (BTG)	Small companies involved in technological and innovative activities	£15,000 to £60,000	Yes	Yes, 10% to 35%	Equity plus preference shares and unsecured loan
Smithdown Investments Tel: (01) 408 1502	Private individuals	Start-up situations and very small companies	£5,000-50,000	Yes	Normally	Open
Stewart Fund Managers Tel: (031) 226 3271	Scottish American Investment, Stewart Enterprise investment	Fast growing companies	£50,000-£500,000	Exceptionally only	Yes, but always minority and can be part of a package	Open
Thamesdale Investment & Finance Co. Ltd Tel: (01) 629 8322	American and European investors	Small/medium sized companies. Equity and loan facilities	£25,000 upwards	Yes, in exceptional circumstances	Yes, 10-40%	Open
Thomson Clive Growth Companies Fund, Thomson Clive Investments Tel: (01) 491 4809	Leading UK institutions	Private companies requiring capital for expansion and having high quality management	£20,000-£300,000	Exceptionally if management of high quality and operations within specific areas of interest	Yes, usually minority	Open
Trust of Property Shares plc Tel: (01) 486 4684	Management support with clearing bankers	Small size private property companies with growth potential requiring capital for expansion	£25,000 to £250,000 Syndicate for larger investments with participation	Possibly, if management of proven calibre	Yes 10-35%	Open

Vehicle for capital	*Backers*	*Type of client or situation*	*Min/Max funds injected*	*Start-up capital*	*Equity stake*	*Term of funding*
UKP-EA Growth Fund Ltd Tel: (01) 831 9991	United Kingdom Provident Institution and the English Association Group plc	Development capital situations. Management buy-outs. Not quoted companies	£50,000-£300,000 but will lead syndicates for larger sums	Only where management has successful track record in related or similar field	Yes, usually up to 30%. Never control	A package tailored to requirement. Loans up to 10 years
Venture Founders Tel: (0295) 65881	British Investment Trusts	Small-medium size growth companies	£50,000-£350,000	Yes	Yes, prefer minority position	Open
Welsh Development Agency Tel: Treforest (0222) 32955	UK Government	Manufacturing and service industries in Wales	£2,000-£1m	Yes	Yes	5-15 years—equity open
Western Enterprise Fund Ltd Tel: (0803) 862271	British Technology Group (BTG) and Dartington & Co. Ltd	Start-ups and small companies with growth potential	Up to £100,000 Syndicate larger investments	Yes	Yes, 10% to 49%	Open
West Midlands Enterprise Board Ltd Tel: (021) 236 8855	West Midlands County Council and various financial institutions	Manufacturing and productive service sector companies employing or likely to employ 100+ in the West Midlands	£100,000-£3m	Yes	Can provide a flexible package of loan/equity capital	Normal financial criteria, but prepared to wait for a long-term capital gain
West Yorkshire Enterprise Board Ltd Tel: Wakefield (0924) 367111	West Yorkshire Metropolitan County Council	Business development; plant modernisation; balance sheet reconstruction; new ventures; management buy-outs	£10,000-£500,000	Yes	Possibly	Medium/long as required

HIRE-PURCHASE AND LEASING

In both cases, the equipment being financed is hired out to the user, rather than bought outright, and in both cases the regular rental payments are fixed at the outset of the contract. The main difference is that under a hire-purchase agreement, ownership of the asset eventually passes to the user, whilst a leased asset remains the property of the lessor (hirer). Often the contract allows the lessee to pay a reduced rent after the end of an agreed period.

Leasing can be particularly appropriate for small firms whose tax situation is such that they cannot benefit from the capital allowances available on the assets being financed. The capital allowance is enjoyed instead by the lessor, who can effectively pass it on to the lessee in the form of reduced rentals. Also the rentals will normally be fully allowable against tax.

FACTORING

Most of the clearing banks have subsidiary or associate companies which specialise in factoring. This is a service based on a book-keeping function but can also mean the provision of finance. There are four main components to factoring:

(a) The administration of the sales ledger; the responsibility for dispatching invoices and ensuring they are paid.

(b) Credit information: the factoring company can provide accurate credit ratings on firms.

(c) The factoring company guarantees payments on approved sales.

(d) Finance: the customer may receive up to 80% of the value of invoices as soon as they are dispatched. Factoring often results in the speedier settlement of trade debts.

EXPORT FINANCE

The clearing banks play a major role in helping firms finance their export sales. The services include facilities for drawing upon documentary credits established by the importer's bankers, as well as financing of the exports themselves, through advances or by discounting the bills that the exporter draws on shipment. The banks also provide advice on the services available from the Export Credits Guarantee Department.

Financial arrangements for exporting differ from domestic business. Finance can be made available to cover the whole cycle of production, shipment and payment by the overseas buyer.

Export finance from a bank may be made on bills of exchange drawn under an export contract. Alternatively bills can be sold outright to a bank or discount house to provide short-term finance.

12 Grant aid schemes

The following list is not exhaustive and can only give brief details of what is currently available. The businessperson should contact the organisation concerned to obtain full details and guidelines. Some schemes have quite rigid application procedures and operate to specific timetables. The schemes do change from time to time and with the current interest in small businesses it is hoped that more schemes will be set up.

UNITED KINGDOM ASSISTED AREAS

In considering the type of financial assistance available, the geographical location of the business is an important factor. A large number of grants currently available to small businesses are dependent on where the business is sited. Of course, the business may already be committed to a particular place because of the type of business being started, the location of its customers, the need to have certain specialist services on hand, or perhaps the firm already has premises which it intends to operate from. Whether this is the case, or whether there is a free choice to start with, is the business eligible for any of the schemes discussed in this section?

One of the first things to establish is whether the business will be located within one of the assisted areas. Figure 1 shows these areas as they are currently defined; if in doubt check with the local office of:

* Department of Industry
* Welsh Office Industry Department
* Scottish Economic Planning Department
* Northern Ireland Department of Economic Development

What are assisted areas?

In order to encourage investment in parts of the UK which have had particular problems of unemployment, the government has designated certain parts of the country as 'areas of expansion', or assisted areas. Under the terms of the Industrial Development Act 1982 and the Local Employment Act 1972 there are special benefits to businesses which move to, or expand or modernise an existing operation within one of the assisted areas.

There are two categories of assisted areas (as from 29 November 1984) and they are, in decreasing order of priority:

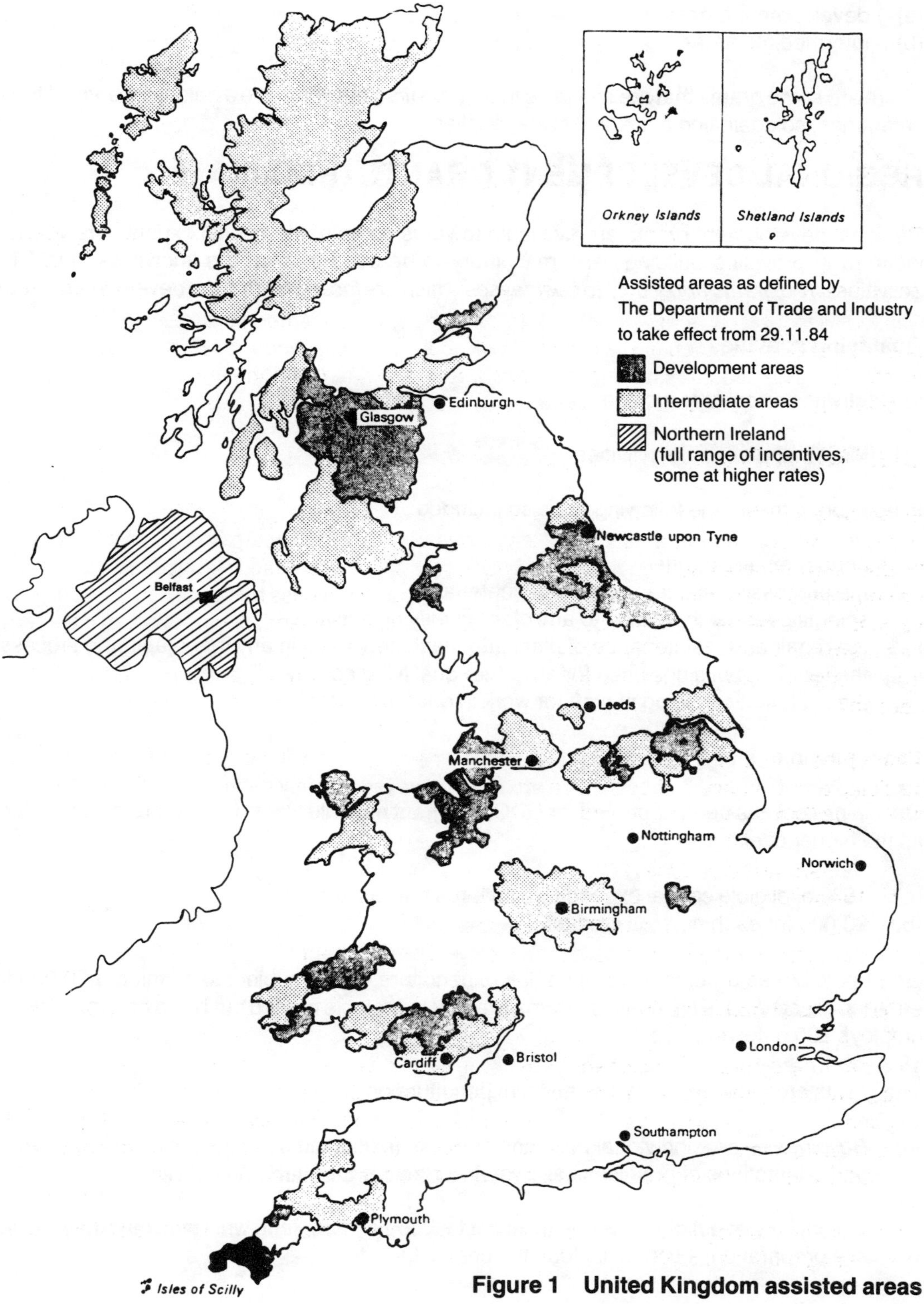

Figure 1 United Kingdom assisted areas

(a) development areas;
(b) intermediate areas.

There are some grants that are available in only the first, but some are available in both, of these categories, so again find out exactly what applies.

REGIONAL DEVELOPMENT GRANTS (RDGs)

Regional development grants are available towards some of the capital expenditure which is incurred in providing buildings and machinery to be used in what are known as 'qualifying activities'. *The grants apply only to businesses which are located within the development areas.*

Qualifying activities

The activities referred to include:

* Most manufacturing activities

In addition to these, the following are also included:

* certain repair activities
* the processing of scrap and waste materials
* scientific research relating to any other qualifying activities
* the repair and maintenance of plant and machinery used in any manufacturing process
* the repair of buildings used for any other qualifying activity
* the systematic training of staff for work in qualifying activities

Grant payable

Once a project has been approved for RDG, the grant payable towards the project is calculated as the higher of either:

(a) 15% of eligible capital expenditure towards new assets; or
(b) £3,000 for each new job created.

Grant payable as a percentage of capital expenditure will be subject to a limit of £10,000 for each job created. This limit will not normally apply to projects carried out by an enterprise which employs 200 or fewer people.

The grants are available towards capital expenditure on:

(a) *Buildings* — new individual buildings or works (excluding mining works), and extensions and adaptations of premises used wholly or mainly for qualifying activities.

The individual building scheme must cost £5,000 or more, and whilst the cost may include site preparation, it cannot include the cost of the site.

(b) *Machinery and plant*— individual items of new plant and machinery costing from £1,000 (£500 in the case of premises where less than 100 people are employed).

Second-hand items are not eligible for a grant, neither are vehicles other than mobile machinery or works vehicles.

Machinery and plant must be used for not less than one year, and have a useful life of at least four years. Things such as furniture, floor coverings, and decorative items are not eligible.

The grant is payable to the purchaser of the item, and this can include a hire-purchaser. Where the asset is being hired, as opposed to being bought, the grant is paid to the owner. There are special arrangements for sale and leaseback. Refer to the regional development grants office *before* applying for a grant.

How to apply

Applications for grants must be received by the appropriate regional development grants office within two years of the end of the quarter in which the asset was provided.

Any other considerations

Capital expenditure on plant and machinery anywhere in the UK qualifies for allowances. Regional development grants are *not* deducted from the cost of the asset when these allowances are computed. In addition to this, these grants are not treated as income receipts for UK tax purposes and so they do not give rise to corporation tax.

Regional development grants are taken into account when considering selective financial assistance (see below), and while this does not affect eligibility for assistance under the scheme, it may influence the amount offered.

SELECTIVE FINANCIAL ASSISTANCE

As well as attracting regional development grants, some businesses may also be eligible for selective financial assistance. Broadly speaking, those *businesses which create or safeguard jobs within the assisted areas* can qualify for further help under s. 7 of the Industrial Development Act 1982. Selective financial assistance is administered by:

(a) Department of Industry;
(b) Scottish Economic Planning Department;
(c) Welsh Office Industry Department.

(See page 167 for selective assistance in Northern Ireland.)

Qualifying activities

Projects which are in the mining, manufacturing and construction industries may be eligible for assistance providing that they can demonstrate the following:

(a) Without the assistance the project could not go ahead in its proposed form, i.e., the provision of assistance must be shown to lead to:

(i) a significant change in the nature or scale of the project;
(ii) a significant advancement in its timing;
(iii) its location within an assisted area (this clause is known as the principle of 'additionality').

From this you can see that a project which has already started is unlikely to qualify, unless it can be shown that the assistance would significantly expand the project.

(b) The project will lead to the creation of additional employment (category A), or will safeguard existing jobs through modernisation (category B).

Under category A the project would be expected to create a specified number of jobs within three years (exceptionally five). If the project only involves the transfer of jobs within assisted areas it is unlikey to qualify unless you can show that it is covered by category B.

(c) The project has a good prospect of being viable, and that the greater part of the finance required is to come from the private sector.

(d) The project will contribute to the national economy, for example by improving productivity, increasing exports.

The effects on the industry as a whole, and on other UK producers, will be taken into consideration.

Grant payable

Selective financial assistance usually takes the form of a grant paid in instalments, related to expenditure on fixed and working capital, and the achievement of the forecast objectives. Grants are discretionary and the amount and the term of assistance is negotiated to provide the minimum amount necessary to enable the project to go ahead.

How to apply

If a project may be eligible under this scheme, contact the Department of Industry for initial discussions. An early indication of whether or not the proposed application is likely to succeed could save a great deal of work in the preparation of the necessary detailed documentation for such an application. No start should be made on a scheme until an offer of assistance has been received.

Any other considerations

Other assistance which has been offered for the project, such as regional development grants, will be taken into account when the amount of selective financial assistance is being decided.

IN-PLANT TRAINING SCHEME

This scheme was introduced to provide assistance towards the training costs which are part of an investment project in either the manufacturing or service industries. In order to qualify, training must be an essential part of the project and a significant element in the cost of the project.

Qualifying activities

To be eligible for a grant the project must satisfy the same criteria as those laid down for selective financial assistance.

Grant payable

The grant covers 40 per cent of eligible training costs, which are:

(a) the basic wages of the trainees;
(b) the instructors; and
(c) cost of materials consumed.

Where training takes place away from the normal place of work, the travel and subsistence expenses of the trainees and instructors may be included.

Training courses may last from 3 to 26 weeks (longer courses will be considered only in exceptional cases).

How to apply

Applications must be approved in advance, and information can be obtained from:

(a) Department of Industry;
(b) Scottish Development Agency;
(c) Welsh Office Industry Department.

Any other considerations

Projects which are eligible under this scheme may also be eligible for a further grant of 40% from the European Community (see p. 178).

GOVERNMENT FACTORIES

Within the *assisted areas* industrial and commercial premises may be available for sale or for rent for projects which create additional employment. In some cases existing businesses whose current premises are unsuitable may be rehoused.

Standard factory units of sizes ranging from small workshops of 500 square feet to buildings of 25,000 square feet, are constructed, and all factories are built to as near a state of completion as possible. To cater for the needs of some of the new high technology industries some sites are being developed on or near to university or polytechnic campuses.

Although not strictly speaking a source of finance (rents are set at commercial levels), a rent-free period of up to two years may be available in some areas. Factories can also be bought, with capital and interest repayments spread over a period of up to 15 years at fixed rates of interest.

Businesses renting or buying government factories may also be eligible for selective financial assistance, in which case they should apply for selective financial assistance before making arrangements to occupy a factory. Any rental concessions will be taken into account when assessing the amount of selective financial assistance to be given.

The factories are managed by:

(a) English Industrial Estate Corporation;
(b) Scottish Development Agency;
(c) Welsh Development Agency.

INVESTMENT IN OFFICE AND SERVICE INDUSTRIES

If the business is part of the service sector as opposed to manufacturing industry, it will not have been eligible for a regional development grant. Selective assistance is available for projects in certain service industries, and this includes commercial, distributive and professional services. Projects which serve a purely local need, e.g., the local corner shop, would not, however, normally be eligible.

Various departments of manufacturing, such as administration, marketing, training, research and development, would also be eligible providing they can be distinguished from the manufacturing activities which they service.

Qualifying activities

In order to qualify for a grant it must be shown that:

(a) The project will create new jobs in an assisted area, either as a result of the business moving into the area, or if it is already established there, by undertaking a new project, or expanding an existing one.

(b) There is a genuine choice of location for the project between an assisted area and elsewhere in the UK. (Some firms which provide certain 'producer service' are exempt from this requirement.)

(c) Without the assistance the project could not go ahead in its proposed form (i.e., the principle of additionality).

Grant payable

The grant is based on the number of new jobs created by the project, and will be the minimum amount necessary for the project to go ahead.

50% of the grant is payable 12 months after the first job is created; the remaining 50% is payable two years later, or on completion of the project, whichever is the sooner. If the number of jobs created is below the number originally forecast, the second payment may be reduced accordingly.

GRANTS TO KEY PERSONNEL

A fixed, non-taxable grant is available towards the expenses of an employee who moves with the firm into an *assisted area*. To be eligible he must have been employed by the firm for six months before the move, and stay with the firm for six months after the move.

Grant payable

The grant of £2,000 is made only if the removal expenses exceed £2,000 and a maximum of 30% of jobs can qualify for this grant.

Grant for feasibility study In order to investigate the possibility of moving to an assisted area it may be necessary to commission a feasibility study from outside consultants. A grant of up to 25% of the consultants' fee (maximum £10,000) is available.

How to apply

Applications for grants must be made, and approval received, before starting the project. Further information about the scheme can be obtained from:

(a) Department of Industry;
(b) Scottish Development Agency;
(c) Welsh Development Agency.

NORTHERN IRELAND

Among the areas considered to have special problems, Northern Ireland is regarded as a special case, and as such, there are a number of incentives available to firms setting up in business there. These incentives are in addition to many of the schemes available in other parts of the UK.

Automatic assistance

Automatic assistance takes the form of grants which are available irrespective of the number of jobs which are to be created by a project. These schemes are administered by the Department of Economic Development.

Capital grants These are similar to regional development grants in that they do not give rise to tax. A grant of 20% of eligible costs of new buildings, plant and machinery used for manufacturing purposes, is available (30% on expenditure incurred before May 1985).

Training grants Where employers provide training for additional workers to fill new jobs, training grants are offered as follows:

(a)	employees aged 18-65	£52 per week
(b)	employees aged under 18	£35 per week

Government factories New or second-hand factories can be bought or leased for industrial or commercial purposes other than retailing.

Rates relief 100% reduction on rates levied on industrial premises.

Key worker grants Where key workers are transferred to Northern Ireland to help set up or expand a business there are cash grants available covering fares, lodging allowances and certain continuing liability expenses.

Selective assistance

Companies in the manufacturing and service industries which undertake new projects or expand existing operations may be eligible for further assistance. These incentives are negotiable, and will be determined by the number of jobs that are to be created.

To qualify for selective assistance, projects must show that:

(a) They have a good prospect of being viable.
(b) They will result in more productive and secure jobs (the 'efficiency' criterion).
(c) They can demonstrate the principle of additionality.

Selective assistance is administered by the Industrial Development Board.

Capital grants The standard automatic assurance capital grant can be increased by negotiation up to a maximum of 50% of eligible capital costs. The rate of grant offered will depend on the location that the company chooses and the employment provided. The tax-free element of the grant is limited to 45% of the eligible cost.

Interest relief grants Grants are made to offset the interest payments made when finance for new developments is raised through loans from non-government sources. Grants are available for up to seven years, up to three years at a broadly commercial rate, followed by four years at 3% p.a.

Rent grants Grants contributing towards rent costs for both government or privately owned premises are available for up to five years.

Start-up grants A substantial cash contribution may be made towards the setting-up cost incurred during the period in which a business is becoming established. This normally takes the form of an employment grant for each job created and is negotiated in relation to the total capital requirement. In addition, there are grants towards managerial costs, including salaries, during this period.

Venture capital Equity participation can be made available to suit the needs of the particular project.

Corporation tax relief grant A corporation tax relief grant of up to 80% will be granted to companies creating new employment. The grant will be available by negotiation and is at the discretion of the Industrial Development Board and the Local Enterprise Development Unit.

Research and development grants Grants of 40-50% are available towards labour and material costs of items such as basic research, related design work, marking and testing of prototypes, final design and production drawing costs. Certain consultancy costs may also be eligible for assistance. Total grant available for any single project is £250,000.

Market research grants Grants of up to 50% of the eligible costs involved in examining potential export markets are available. Eligible costs include consultants' fees and expenses, researchers' travel costs plus an allowance for in-house research and the purchase of market research or special marketing studies.

Further information For further information about any of these schemes you should contact the following:

Department of Economic Development,
Netherleigh,
Massey Ave,
Belfast BT4 2JP
Tel: Belfast 63244

Industrial Development Board for Northern Ireland,
IDB House,
64 Chichester St,
Belfast BT1 4JX
Tel: Belfast 233233

Industrial Development Board for Northern Ireland,
Ulster Office,
11 Berkeley St,
London W1X 6BU
Tel: (01) 493 0601

Local Enterprise Development Unit

This is the small business agency for Northern Ireland and its basic aim is to promote the establishment of small local manufacturing and service industries employing less than 50 people. It does not normally assist wholesale, retail, distribution, tourist and transport operations, or industries not suited to small-scale activities.

The Local Enterprise Development Unit can assist by making available:

* loans and grants geared to the needs of each project

* advice and practical help with marketing, accountancy and management problems

* a business centre for promotions and exhibitions, small business counselling and a licensing library

For further information on this unit you should contact:

LEDU,
Lamont House,
Purdy's Lane,
Newtonbreda,
Belfast BT8 4TB
Tel: Belfast 691031

RURAL AREAS IN ENGLAND

The Development Commission

The Development Commission was established in 1909 to assist the English rural areas. In particular, the eight commissioners advise the government on the spending of the development fund, a sum voted annually by parliament. The main aims of the Commission are to reduce rural depopulation, improve the economic and social structure of the rural areas, and to create employment.

In setting out these objectives the government recognised that some areas of the country were particularly disadvantaged, and designated these as *special investment areas*. While, technically speaking, any scheme that would benefit the rural economy is eligible for assistance if no other statutory assistance is available, the Commission has concentrated the bulk of its resources on certain activities in the special investment areas.

These activities can be summarised into the following main categories:

* Providing small factories and workshops in partnership with local authorities, both by building new units and by converting existing buildings.

* Providing assistance to small rural industries through the funding of the Council for Small Industries in Rural Areas (CoSIRA).

* Encouraging voluntary organisations such as the Rural Community Council, the National Council for Voluntary Organisations, and the National Federation of Women's Institutes, which enrich the social and cultural life of the rural areas.

Council for Small Industries in Rural Areas (CoSIRA)

From the point of view of small business, this is the most important aspect of the Development Commission's work. The Council for Small Industries in Rural Areas was established in 1968, and its job is to assist small firms employing not more than 20 skilled people in rural areas and country towns with a population of less than 10,000. In March 1987, CoSIRA was servicing some 27,413 rural small firms employing 116,000 people. Of the firms assisted, 7,000 were new starters.

Loans CoSIRA has its own loan fund for small industries and small tourist projects (agriculture, horticulture and the professions are not eligible).

The maximum loan available is £75,000, minimum £250, and this can cover up to 50% of the project cost of buildings, plant and equipment. Loans for buildings are made over a period of 20 years, and for plant and equipment over 2-5 years; interest rates are specified by the Treasury and vary according to the term of the loan.

In addition to this CoSIRA have an agreement with the National Westminster Bank and Barclays Bank to enable clients to borrow up to £250,000 for buildings, plant and equipment.

Under a pilot scheme CoSIRA has been able to offer grants of up to 35% towards the conversion of redundant farm buildings in the uplands. The Commission hopes to extend this scheme throughout the special investment areas, and to all suitable buildings.

Designation of rural development areas

The Commission and CoSIRA have concentrated the bulk of their resources in the special investment areas designated by the government. Following a recent review the Commissioners are, in future, to designate their own priority areas, and these will be known as rural development areas.

In deciding upon these areas the Commission will take into account such factors as:

* above average unemployment, and poor employment opportunities
* population decline, and the outward migration of people of working age
* imbalance in the age structure towards elderly people
* poor access to services and facilities

All the rural development areas were designated at the same time, in the first half of 1984.

Further information Further information is available from:

The Development Commission,
11 Cowley St,
London SW1P 3NA
Tel: (01) 222 9134

CoSIRA
141 Castle St,
Salisbury,
Wiltshire SP1 1EX
Tel: (0722) 6255

SCOTLAND

The Scottish Development Agency

As the name implies, the Scottish Development Agency is concerned with the promotion of the economic development of Scotland. Its objectives are to create and safeguard employment, increase industrial efficiency and international competitiveness, and to improve the environment. In order to achieve these aims, the Development Agency can give assistance in the form of loans, guarantees, share capital, industrial and financial partnerships, factories and management advisory services.

Whilst the Agency is prepared to consider any project in Scotland which comes within its general guidelines, the sorts of project which are most likely to be assisted are:

* Projects already in Scotland, or about to be established there, which plan to enter new markets or develop new techniques.

* Expansion projects by enterprise in Scotland.

* Companies in Scotland which have a good prospect of long-term profitability but which are experiencing short-term difficulties.

* Projects which will assist the economic regeneration of local economies.

Small business division This division of the Agency can provide medium and long-term loans of £1,000 to £150,000 to small businesses in the manufacturing and service industries employing less than 100 people. The loans are generally for the following periods:

Plant, machinery, equipment, working capital	5 years
Buildings	20 years

Security is usually required. Interest rates are fixed and will normally be at commercial levels. However, if the project will create additional employment in a rural area there may be some possibility of it being granted a concessionary rate.

In addition to providing finance, the small business division also offers other services which may be of benefit:

* general counselling services
* advice on marketing, exporting, production organisation, materials, equipment, subcontracting
* advice on financial management

(There may be a small charge for some of these services.)

The Scottish Development Agency acts as an agent to the European Investment Bank and the European Coal and Steel Community and can make their loans available to businesses in Scotland.

Manufacturing businesses which create employment for redundant coal and steel workers in an area affected by closures can qualify for loans to cover 50% of the fixed capital costs of the project. Loans are given for a period of eight years, at fixed interest rates, with a four-year repayment 'holiday'. These loans are only available to firms with up to 50 employees. For businesses which do not qualify under the small business division's schemes the Development Agency can arrange loans for up to 20 years at competitive interest rates. There is no upper limit to the amount, but security will usually be required. The Development Agency may also be prepared to give guarantees on suitable terms, to enable businesses to borrow money from other sources.

Finance provided by the Scottish Development Agency is regarded as coming from the private sector, and therefore does not affect the regional assistance available under the assisted areas scheme.

Further information Information on the above, including the small business division, can be obtained from:

Information Department,
Scottish Development Agency,
120 Bothwell St,
Glasgow G2 7JP
Tel: (041) 248 2700

Highlands and Islands Development Board

This government agency was established in 1965 to assist the economic and social development of the Scottish highlands and islands.

The Board can provide finance in the form of loans, grants and equity for a wide range of developments in the following areas: the Highland region, the Western Isles, Shetland, Orkney, and the Strathclyde region, Argyll and Bute District, the Isle of Arran and Cumbrae.

Projects moving from non-development areas into one of the above may qualify for a grant of 80 per cent of removal costs.

The types of project which the Board is prepared to consider for assistance include those in the manufacturing industry, craft, tourist facilities, agriculture and fishing.

Finance The amount available in loans and grants is discretionary and will depend upon such factors as location and the employment created. The Board is able to offer 50% of the total cost of establishing the project, the other half being provided by the entrepreneur from his own resources or from commercial borrowing. In exceptional circumstances the Board can provide up to 70% of the finance required.

Loans are provided for up to 10 years for plant, machinery and working capital, and for up to 20 years for buildings. Rates of interest are fixed and may be below commercial levels. Although security is usually required, the Board has the discretionary power to waive this for loans of up to £6,000.

As an alternative to giving loans, the Board can make available interest relief grants to reduce the interest costs of borrowing from other sources. 'Special grants' are available for projects which the Board considers have particular significance, and which could not go ahead without additional help. These grants are normally of up to 20% of the project's costs (in exceptional cases this can be extended to 50% where the project cost is less than £60,000).

The usual regional development grants are available throughout most of the islands and highlands, and the Board would expect them to be taken up. Such grants will be taken into account when determining the level of assistance to be given by the Highlands and Islands Board.

Other services provided by the Board include:

(a) *Social development grants* Grants of up to £15,000 are available towards projects that meet social needs and contribute to social development.

(b) *Training grants* New companies or existing businesses which recruit new staff may be eligible for grants of up to 50% of the identifiable training costs.

(c) *Factories* Standard and custom built factories are available at favourable rents, and in some cases rent-free for up to two years.

(d) *Advisory services* The Board provides an advisory service which can cover such subjects as marketing, production engineering, management accounting, recruitment and training.

Further information The address of the Highlands and Islands Development Board is:

The Highlands and Islands Development Board,
Bridge House,
Bank St,
Inverness IV1 1QR
Tel: 0463 234171

Clydesdale Enterprise Fund

New business setting up within the area covered by the Clydesbank enterprise zone are eligible for loans from this Fund. It provides unsecured risk finance for loans of up to £25,000 at a rate of interest of 5%.

Local enterprise grants for urban projects

The first assistance to projects in deprived urban areas was announced in September 1982. Any type of project bringing benefit to a deprived urban area and demonstrating additionality will be considered. The Scottish Development Agency administers the schemes.

WALES

Mid Wales Development

The Mid Wales Development offers finance, business advice and other services to encourage firms to set up or expand their operations in Wales.

The areas it covers are:

Dyfed: Ceredigion
Gwynedd: Merionnydd
Powys: Brecknock; Montgomery; Radnor

The Mid Wales Development can offer the following:

Rural loans Loans of up to £75,000 are available to firms employing less than 20 skilled people, the loans being dependent on the creation of sufficient new jobs. Interest rates are fixed, and are at approximately 3% below commercial rates. Security is normally required.

Standard loans Loans ranging from £2,500 to £500,000 are available for projects at commercial fixed interest rates. The loans are available for buildings, plant and machinery, and working capital, with repayment terms of 5-20 years. Priority is given to manufacturing industry, and projects within the transport, distribution, construction, agriculture and retail sectors are not eligible.

Equity finance can also be provided, usually as part of a package including standard loans.

Applications must be made before the start of the project.

Wage subsidy Small firms (employing 25 people or less) may obtain a wage subsidy of up to 30% of the basic wage on up to five new jobs. The jobs must be filled by previously unemployed people, and the subsidy is paid for 26 weeks. The subsidy is at the discretion of the local council.

Mid Wales development grants Grants are available for projects in the manufacturing, commercial, construction and service industries which create or safeguard jobs in areas which lose their assisted area status. The criteria for grants are similar to those for selective assistance in assisted areas, and projects must show that without the grant the scheme could not go ahead. It follows, therefore, that applications should be made before the start of the project.

Factories Factories of between 500 and 20,000 square feet are available in many towns, and rent-free periods may be negotiated depending on the area. Some local authorities offer rate concessions.

A business advisory service gives guidance on marketing, promotions, accountancy and setting up in business.

Welsh Development Agency

The Welsh Development Agency was established in 1976 to help regenerate the Welsh economy by providing investment funds, factories and advisory services to assist both new and existing industries.

Loans Investment capital in the form of equity funds and loans is provided, and financial packages are designed to meet the needs of individual businesses. All sectors of industry, with the exception of property development, financial businesses and service industries meeting only a local need, are eligible.

Loans are made on commercial terms, usually for a period of 5-10 years, at fixed rates of interest. Deferment of capital repayments can be arranged, and security is usually required. Small businesses which create new jobs in rural areas may qualify for loans at reduced rates of interest. It is the Agency's policy to limit its shareholdings to 30% of the equity of any company, and it negotiates buy-back arrangements for the subsequent disposal of holdings on agreed terms.

Hafren Investment Finance Ltd Hafren Investment Finance is a venture capital subsidiary of the Development Agency which specialises in providing risk funds for new technology projects and young companies with a high growth potential. £10,000-£200,000 is available per business, and Hafren will allow an early buy-out of its stake on terms agreed at the start.

Further information This is available from:

Mid Wales Development,
Ladywell House,
Newtown,
Powys SY16 1JB
Tel: 0686 26965

Small business unit The small business unit of the Agency provides management and technical advice to small firms. These services are charged for on a sliding scale according to company size.

Other services

* *Factories* The Welsh Development Agency builds standard and custom built factories ranging from 380 to 50,000 square feet.
* *General advice* The Development Agency can provide information and advice on grants and loans available to businesses in Wales. Information on labour, materials, suppliers, housing, etc. is also available.

European assistance The Development Agency acts as an agent for the European Investment Bank and the European Coal and Steel Community. Low interest loans are available to businesses in the assisted areas, and to manufacturing firms in the areas affected by closures in the coal and steel sectors.

Further information This is available from:

Welsh Development Agency
Pearl House,
Greyfriars Rd,
Cardiff CF1 3XX
Tel: 0222 32955

13 European Economic Community funds

The Community's budget provides for a number of funds which are designed to promote the Community's objectives by financing suitable projects. Such funds include the social fund and the regional development fund. In addition to these, there are specialised Community institutions such as the European Investment Bank (EIB), which provides finance in the form of grants and low interest loans for projects mainly in the industrial, energy and infrastructure fields.

The regulations governing the operations of these funds and institutions can be complex, and are designed to ensure that the finance is used to achieve the objectives of the Community. As the Community's policies and objectives change, the regulations are reviewed and updated. Additionally, the money allocated to these funds has to be voted by the member states each year, and consequently the amount of cash available can vary.

However, the EEC could be a very useful source of finance to consider, and businesses should not be put off by the apparent remoteness of Brussels. A number of schemes which are likely to be of most interest to the small business are administered by local institutions acting as agents for the Community.

THE EUROPEAN INVESTMENT BANK (EIB)

The European Investment Bank was established to provide funds in the form of loans and guarantees for capital investment projects in industry, energy, tourism or related infrastructure or services.

To do this the EIB raises money on the world's money markets and then on-lends these funds at fixed interest rates. Because of its status as a borrower it is able to obtain money at the best rates, and can offer loans at advantageous rates of interest.

Prior to 1985 the EIB made 'global' loans to banks and other financial institutions for them to on-lend. Since then only loans negotiated directly between the EIB and the prospective borrower have been available. The lower limit of the loans is usually £1.5 million.

Eligibility for loans

A project may be eligible for assistance if it:

(a) promotes regional development in the *assisted areas*; or
(b) serves a common interest of several member states or the Community as a whole; or
(c) leads to the modernisation or conversion of industries to overcome structural problems.

The majority of the loans are made for industrial investment, the development of energy supplies (particularly those which reduce the EEC's dependence on oil imports), and the improvement of public infrastructure.

EXCHANGE RISK GUARANTEE SCHEME

Loans from the EIB and the European Coal and Steel Community (ECSC) are usually made in foreign currencies. In order to cover private sector borrowers against the risk of exchange losses the UK government operates an Exchange Risk Guarantee Scheme.

Projects which meet the criteria for regional selective financial assistance are eligible for the scheme, whereby the government takes the risk in return for an annual premium, and the borrower's liability is fixed in sterling.

EUROPEAN SOCIAL FUND

The European Social Fund is essentially concerned with employment and training, and operates by giving financial support in the form of grants to training schemes which meet specified conditions. A grant from the Social Fund to a private sector company can match, but not exceed, assistance already being provided by a public authority. In general, assistance is given for the running costs of the schemes, and will not cover capital expenditure.

Following the recent review of the work of the Fund it seems clear that the bulk of its resources will be directed towards assisting schemes which will promote employment for young people under 25, whose chances of employment are particularly poor through lack of training, or who are long-term unemployed.

Applications to the Fund should be channelled through the Department of Employment, which will provide guidelines and application forms.

The Fund is heavily oversubscribed and not all eligible schemes will necessarily receive funding.

EUROPEAN COAL AND STEEL COMMUNITY (ECSC)

Funds from the ECSC are made available to projects which promote the modernisation of the coal and steel industries, and which provide employment opportunities for redundant coal and steel workers.

Conversion loans

Firms in the manufacturing industries which undertake projects which will create employment opportunities for redundant coal and steel workers may qualify for grants of up to 50% of the fixed capital costs of the project. To be eligible the firm does not have to be related to the coal and steel industries, but must be located within an affected area. This is usually taken to mean within a radius of 10-15 miles of a steel works or coal mine where there have been redundancies.

Loans are made at fixed rates of interest, usually for a term of eight years. Capital repayment holidays can be arranged, and interest relief of up to 3% p.a. may be granted, depending on the number of jobs created and the location. Exchange risk cover can be arranged.

Applications for a grant must be made before work starts on a project, and details can be obtained from the local office of:

* Department of Trade and Industry, Tel: (01) 212 3395
* Scottish Economic Planning Department, Tel: (041) 248 2855
* Welsh Office Industry Department, Tel: (0222) 825111
* Northern Ireland — Department of Economic Planning, Tel: (0232) 34488

How to apply

For loans of £4 million or more application should be made via the Department of Trade and Industry.

For loans of up to £1 million application should be made to:

* Industrial and Commercial Finance Corporation
* Scottish Development Agency
* Welsh Development Agency
* Clearing banks

Industrial loans

Loans similar to the above can be given to projects involving investment in plant, machinery and buildings which reflect Community policy for coal and steel. Any project which assists the use of coal and steel, e.g., by increasing production, reducing costs, can be eligible and finance is not restricted to the coal and steel industries themselves.

Application should be made as indicated above.

Housing loans

Loans at low rates of interest are available for improving the housing conditions of workers in the coal and steel industries, both for new construction and modernisation.

The maximum loan for first time buyers is 20% of the purchase cost, up to 25% for transferees, and up to 40% for improvements. The cost of the loans is 1-2% including a commission to the building society which operated the scheme for the Commission.

Applications for the loans are made via employers, and further details can be obtained from:

European Communities Commission,
Information Office,
8 Storey's Gate,
London SW1P 3AT
Tel: (01) 222 8122

Other assistance

Grants for research in the coal and steel industry are available for technical, economic, social and medical research projects.

Grants to coal and steel workers affected by fundamental changes in market conditions can be given to help resettlement in other regions and training.

Further information can be obtained from the above address.

EUROPEAN REGIONAL DEVELOPMENT FUND (ERDF)

The ERDF was established in 1975 to assist regional development. 'The quota' section of the fund is used to assist projects in industry, tourism, service activities and infrastructure within the assisted areas. The project must also be receiving funds from the UK Government.

The Department of Trade and Industry and its equivalents in Scotland, Wales and Northern Ireland administer the scheme.

Assistance is limited to 5% of the ERDF's total resources. Contributions will not exceed 50% of the total amount of regional aid granted by public authorities, provided at least 10 jobs are created or maintained.

The 'non-quota' section can provide assistance to small and medium sized firms (manufacturing firms with less than 200 employees, other firms with less than 25) who are engaged in certain activities within areas affected by the restructuring of the steel and shipbuilding areas. The areas affected are: Strathclyde, Cleveland, Tyne and Wear, Merseyside, Corby, Clwyd, South Glamorgan, Gwent and Belfast.

The activities eligible for assistance include:

* provision of consultancy and common service
* promoting technological innovation, providing information or innovation
* facilitating access to risk capital

Details of assistance available should be sought from:

Department of Industry,
Regional Policy and Development Grants Division,
Kingsgate House,
66-74 Victoria St,
London SW1E 6SJT
Tel: (01) 212 0400

EUROPEAN ENERGY SECTOR FUNDS

The European Community has allocated funds for the promotion of more efficient energy installation and for the encouragement of a higher level of technological innovation.

Assistance is available for projects in the following fields:

* nuclear energy
* hydrocarbons
* uranium prospecting
* alternative energy
* energy-saving projects

Details of these schemes can be obtained from the European Community Commission.

14 Local forms of assistance

GRANTS FROM LOCAL AUTHORITIES

A local authority can be a very useful source of finance and it is one that is frequently overlooked, so it is worthwhile contacting them to find out what sort of assistance they can offer. Because they vary considerably in the scope and type of scheme which they offer, it is possible to give only a broad outline here; fuller information may be obtained by asking the local authority to send any pamphlets or publications on local schemes.

All local authorities have certain general powers to provide assistance to industry where this is in the local interest. These powers include the giving of mortgage loans of up to 90% for buying land, or carrying out works on land; with the permission of the Secretary of State they may dispose of land at below its market value (this is only done in exceptional circumstances); and local authorities may invest monies from their pension funds in local businesses.

Within the guidelines laid down by the various statutes, the local authorities are able to set their own priorities in allocating resources, and this means that the amount of money available differs from area to area. The criteria by which applications for assistance are assessed will also be given different rights by the individual authorities according to their priorities, so it is important to be aware of the particular policies of the authority covering the area in which a business is seeking to become established.

In addition to the general powers described above many local authorities have obtained additional powers through Private Acts of Parliament. These powers enable them to draw up their own schemes to assist local businesses, and there is a wide variety of such schemes available throughout the UK. It is impossible to list the individual schemes here due to their number and complexity, but the local town hall should be able to provide information on any such schemes.

The most common local authority schemes cover the following

* Wage subsidies and grants given to firms recruiting the unemployed: subsidies are usually available for a specified length of time, and the authority will have guidelines on how long the recruit must have been unemployed to qualify and the minimum number of hours per week he must work to be eligible.

* Factories: local authorities are often able to provide premises with subsidised rents, or short-term leases. Premises such as workshops suitable for small enterprises are being made available in increasing numbers.

* Loans and grants for working capital: most local authority finance is specifically reserved for providing premises. However, some authorities have schemes for plant and working capital, and these usually take the form of loans of up to 90% of the cost.

* Relocation grants: some authorities provide grants towards the cost of relocation, usually with a maximum of £2,000.

* Start-up and small business schemes: start-up schemes often take the form of a package including loans, guarantees, workshop facilities. Small business schemes are designed to encourage small businesses. (Local authority definitions of 'small business' vary, usually between 5 and 10 people) and grants available are up to about £2,000.

Inner urban areas

Section 1 of the Inner Urban Areas Act 1978 defines certain districts which are known as *designated districts*. These are areas which have had special 'inner city' problems, and local authorities at county, borough and district levels are empowered to provide additional financial assistance to businesses in those areas. Priority is usually given to manufacturing industry, but projects from the service sector may also be considered.

Qualifying activities

Before giving assistance under these schemes a local authority would have to be satisfied that a business would:

(a) benefit the economic development of the particular area;
(b) be viable, and either create or preserve jobs;
(c) where appropriate, lead to improvements in either property or the environment;
(d) not be able to obtain the necessary finance from other sources.

Assistance available

* Loans of up to 90% of the secured value (i.e., mortgage loans) for buying land and for carrying out building and site works. Loans are available for up to 30 years at commercial rates of interest.

* Grants or loans of up to £1,000 towards the costs of setting up cooperatives or common ownership enterprises. This can only cover the administrative costs, e.g., registration fees, professional advice, but not capital or running costs.

* A local authority can declare certain places 'improvement areas' in order to provide loans and grants for improvements to amenities in commercial or industrial areas which would otherwise decline due to poor buildings and environment

* Grants are available covering 50% of the cost of converting, improving and modernising commercial and industrial buildings.

Some of the designated districts have 'inner city partnership areas' within which are certain defined areas, known as 'special areas', where the local authority can provide additional assistance:

* Interest-free loans for up to two years for site preparation and the installation of services.

* Grants towards the interest being paid by firms employing less than 50 people on loans made for the purpose of buying land or buildings.

To be eligible the firm must have been trading in the special area for 12 months, and the maximum grant is 12% of the amount borrowed. The grant can be paid in instalments over up to four years, but cannot amount to more than 6% of the total sum borrowed in any one year.

The individual authorities can set the terms and conditions of the assistance that they offer. Generally speaking, interest rates on loans are usually at commercial rates and security will be required. Assistance may be made conditional on certain employment creation targets being met, or standards of wages or working conditions being achieved.

How to apply

Application procedures are laid down by the individual authorities, from whom guidance should be sought on the correct way to apply. Because of the variations between the local authorities, both in interpretation and implementation of the schemes, it is advisable to contact them as soon as practicable to get an indication of whether a particular project is likely to be given consideration.

ENTERPRISE ZONES

Enterprise zones were originally created as an experiment to assess to what extent industrial and commercial activity would be encouraged by the lifting of certain tax burdens, and the relaxation of some administrative and statutory controls. New and existing businesses within the designated zones can benefit from the following concessions:

* exemption from rates on industrial and commercial property

* 100% allowances for income and corporation tax purposes on industrial and commercial property

* simplification of planning procedures

* government requests for statistical information will be reduced to a minimum

* exemption from Industrial Training Board levies as well as any requirements to supply them with information.

The special incentives in enterprise zones are in addition to whatever other benefits may be available under other schemes, e.g., assisted area schemes.

The areas currently designated as enterprise zones are:

England: Corby, Dudley, Glanform, Hartlepool, Isle of Dogs, Tyneside/Gateshead, Spele, Salford/Trafford, Wakefield, Wellingborough, Workington, Middlesbrough, North-East Lancashire, North-West Kent, Rotherham, Scunthorpe, Telford.

Scotland: Clydebank, Invergordon, Tayside.

Wales: Lower Swansea Valley, Delyn, Milford Haven Waterway.

Northern Ireland: Belfast, Londonderry.

URBAN DEVELOPMENT CORPORATIONS

Two urban development corporations have been set up in the dockland areas of London and Merseyside to assist in the regeneration of these areas. They have been given special powers to undertake programmes of land acquisition and infrastructure provision in order to attract sector development.

Their powers to provide loans and grants are similar to those of the local authorities in the designated districts.

Further information on these corporations is available from:

Business Research and Information Centre,
Dockmasters House,
West India Dock Rd,
London E14 8JX
Tel: (01) 515 2020

Merseyside Development Corporation
Royal Liver Buildings,
Pier Head,
Liverpool L3 1JE
Tel: (051) 236 6090

TOURISM

Discretionary assistance for projects which provide or improve tourist facilities throughout the UK are available from the English, Welsh and Scottish Tourist Boards. Each Board has its own priorities and operates its own schemes so the assistance available will vary.

In general terms, the Board will be prepared to consider projects which will attract more tourists both from Britain and from abroad, will increase tourist spending, and will create employment directly or indirectly.

The assistance is available towards capital cost only, and projects must have already been granted outline planning permission, where required. To qualify for a grant you must be able to demonstrate that your project is viable, and that it could not go ahead in its proposed form without the assistance, i.e., additionality. The level of assistance will be limited to the minimum amount necessary to enable the project to proceed.

Grants can be of up to 50% of the capital cost of the project, although in practice they are usually in the region of 15-20%.

To encourage greater private sector finance the Tourist Boards also offer interest relief grants for tourist development projects. These grants reduce the cost of borrowing for up to three years (exceptionally four years), and are currently as follows:

first and second years	11%
third and fourth years	3%

The relief grants can provide for borrowings of up to 50% of the costs for new projects, and up to 75% of the costs of extensions to existing businesses.

For small hotels, guest houses, etc., in certain rural areas and country towns in the special development and development areas, and in the Development Commission's special investment areas, loans may be available from the Council for Small Industries in Rural Areas (CoSIRA).

Assistance for a project can be a combination of the above grants and loans from other public funds, but the total assistance given cannot exceed 50% of the total capital costs. Any assistance in excess of £50,000 (currently under review) must first be approved by the Department of Trade, the Welsh Office or the Scottish Economic Planning Department, and the Treasury.

The Tourist Boards act as agents for the European Investment Bank (EIB) and projects in the assisted areas may be eligible for loans of up to £2.5 million.

The Highlands and Islands Development Board also provides assistance to tourist projects within its region.

The addresses of the Tourist Board are as follows:

English Tourist Board,
24 Grosvenor Gardens,
London SW1W 0ET
Tel: (01) 730 3400

Scottish Tourist Board,
23 Ravelston Terrace,
Edinburgh EH4 3EU
Tel: (031) 332 2433

Welsh Tourist Board,
Brunel House,
2 Fitzalan Rd,
Cardiff CF2 1UY
Tel: (0222) 499909

15 Research, development and technology

In recent years there has been an increasing emphasis on the need for investment in research and development, particularly that related to the new technologies.

DEPARTMENT OF TRADE AND INDUSTRY NATIONWIDE SCHEMES

The Department of Trade and Industry is encouraging innovation and the exploitation of new technology with a number of special schemes designed to promote the use of computers, microprocessors and fibre-optics. As well as providing general advice and expert knowledge, some of these schemes offer financial assistance towards equipment and project costs. However, these schemes are subject to changes partly due to the rapid advancement of modern technology and finite funding, and it is advisable to check with local offices of the Department of Trade and Industry should there be any problems. The information given in this part of the book is accurate at the time the book went to print (December 1987).

SUPPORT FOR INNOVATION

The aim of this scheme is to help companies in or closely associated with any UK manufacturing industry to put new or significantly improved products on the market quickly and more effectively. Projects which involve innovation in traditional sectors as well as those dealing with new technology are eligible for assistance under this scheme.

To be eligible for support it must be shown that:

(a) The company has the managerial, commercial, financial and technical ability to carry the project through.

(b) The development has a good prospect of success.

(c) Without the government assistance the project could not proceed in its proposed form, i.e., additionality.

Support will be given throughout the development, from the design stage to the launch, and the eligible costs will be the attributable labour, materials and overhead costs incurred up to the point of commercial production. These costs include consultancy fees, design costs and prototypes.

The cost of the project should normally fall into the range £25,000 to £5 million. However, small firms are encouraged to submit plans costing below the £25,000. Any other government assistance being provided towards the project, e.g., regional development grant, will be deducted from eligible costs before an offer of assistance under this scheme is made.

Approval must be obtained before the work is commenced; no retrospective assistance will be given.

The support can take the following forms:

Grants

Grants of up to 25% of the eligible costs can be given.

Shared cost contracts

For longer-term projects, and usually only in exceptional circumstances, the Department of Industry may participate in a shared cost contract where it will bear up to 50% of the eligible costs. This investment is recovered by a levy on commercial sales.

Pre-production models

Under a pre-production order agreement the Department of Industry may purchase up to four pre-production models which embody the new techniques, and will place these with potential users for evaluation.

The trial period usually lasts for one year, at the end of which the user is expected to buy the product if it is satisfactory. If the product is not satisfactory the Department will expect the manufacturer to buy back the equipment at an agreed price, allowing for depreciation.

The orders should normally total between £25,000 and £1.25 million, but again, orders of less than £25,000 will be welcomed from small firms.

Applicants for this support will be expected to explain why adequate sales and trials cannot be achieved without government aid.

Further information Further details are available from either:

Information Technology Division,
Department of Trade and Industry,
Kingsgate House,
66-74 Victoria St,
London SW1E 6SW
Tel: (01) 215 7877

or

Electronics Applications Divisions,
Department of Trade and Industry,
Kingsgate House,
66-74 Victoria St,
London SW1E 6SW
Tel: (01) 215 8002

JOINT APPRAISAL SCHEME

Companies which apply for government aid towards research and development costs may also be seeking funds from banks and other financial institutions. Where the Department of Trade and Industry has made an offer of assistance under the Support for Innovation Scheme, it will make its technical appraisal of the project available to financial institutions to help in the assessment of possible cooperation in the joint promotion of the project.

COMPUTER-AIDED DESIGN/COMPUTER-AIDED MANUFACTURING (CADCAM)

The Government has recognised that the computer has a great potential for increasing productivity and competitiveness, and in 1982 it launched an awareness campaign to accelerate the acceptance and application of computer aids to design, draughting, planning, estimating and manufacturing. CADCAM is directed principally at the engineering sector, particularly mechanical engineering.

Under this scheme the following assistance is available to firms.

Support for consultancy studies

A grant of up to £2,500 is available on a selective basis towards the cost of a consultant to investigate the economic or technical feasibility of using computer aids. Grants are limited to one per firm, and the Department of Industry must approve the choice of consultant and the CADCAM project before the study commences.

Support for product and process development

Grants are available on the same terms as Support for Innovation (see above).

Demonstration firms

Firms with CADCAM installations who are willing to demonstrate their systems to potential users may receive support.

Other assistance

This includes:

* Managers' awareness seminars: one-day CADCAM seminars including case studies and discussions with a consultant for managing directors.

* In-depth courses: one-week courses to help design managers and production managers plan their firm's approach to the technology.

* Practical experience centres: CADCAM centres provide facilities so that key staff from potential users can study techniques and try out the equipment.

* CADCAM information point: an information point is being set up to provide information on equipment, suppliers, software, courses, etc.

Further information Information on CADCAM can be obtained from any Department of Trade and Industry Regional Office, or:

Department of Trade and Industry,
MEE2 Branch, Room 401,
Ashdown House,
123 Victoria St,
London SW1E 6RB
Tel: (01) 212 5789

CADMAT

In the production of computers and electronic equipment, there are specialist requirements for the design, verification, layout and interconnection of circuits, and for manufacture, procurement and testing. The computer-aided techniques designed to satisfy these requirements are known as CADMAT. The CADMAT programme is designed with extending and accelerating the use of the CADMAT by small and medium sized firms in mind, and is directed mainly at the electronics industry.

Capital support grants

First-time users of modern CADMAT equipment can apply for a grant of up to 25% towards the cost of hardware, software, installation and the training of personnel, where such a grant will accelerate the introduction of the equipment. Software houses or bureaux which provide direct design or test support to the manufacturing industry may also be eligible for support.

Further information Further details on the above grants may be obtained from:

Electronics Applications Division,
Department of Trade and Industry,
Kingsgate House,
66-74 Victoria St,
London SW1E 6SW
Tel: (01) 215 8002

Other assistance

This includes:

* Seminars for management: Seminars for top management organised by the Institution of Electrical Engineers to promote awareness of CADMAT.

* Short courses: two-day courses to give managers and engineers a knowledge of the basic need to use CADMAT.

* Demonstrations: major users of CADMAT are to put on demonstrations to show how the system works in the actual industrial environment.

* Information service: The Department of Industry has set up an information service on all aspects of the technology for the benefit of existing and prospective CADMAT users.

Further information Further details on these services are available from:

The Institution of Electrical Engineers
Savoy Place
London WC2R 0BL
Tel: (01) 240 1871

COMPUTER-AIDED DESIGN AND TEST EQUIPMENT (CADTES)

Assistance with capital equipment purchases in support of computer-aided design, manufacture and test schemes can be provided to first-time users of computer aided application. The eligible costs include any mixture of hardware and software purchase or leasing cost (four-year minimum lease) plus an allowance of up to 15% for training and installation costs.

The grant of up to 25% of the eligible costs is subject to a maximum of £60,000 to any one firm. There is no lower limit for firms employing up to 200 people; larger firms are subject to a minimum of £6,000.

Further information Notes for the guidance of applicants can be obtained from:

Electronics Applications Division,
Department of Trade and Industry,
Kingsgate House,
66-74 Victoria St,
London SW1E 6SW
Tel: (01) 215 8002

SOFTWARE PRODUCTS SCHEME

This scheme was established in 1973 to encourage the development of software products and packages and their practical application in key technological areas. Any UK-based software company, bureau or consultancy can apply for a grant of up to 25% of the cost of developing and marketing the product in the first two years. Proposals can be for a new product or for the further development of an existing one.

Further information This is available from:

The Software Products Scheme Administrator,
National Computing Centre Ltd,
Bracken House,
Charles St,
Manchester M1 7BD
Tel: (061) 228 6333

TELECOM PRODUCTS SCHEME

This scheme provides grants for product development and capital equipment and applies to equipment designed to be attached to the public telecommunications networks. It is aimed particularly at small to medium sized firms and grants of up to 25% for development, and negotiable grants for capital equipment, are available, where the total project cost does not exceed £3 million.

Applications must be received within six months of government approval of the appropriate BSI standard.

Further information This may be obtained from:

Department of Trade and Industry,
Information Technology Division,
Kingsgate House,
66-74 Victoria St,
London SW1E 6SW
Tel: (01) 215 7877

MICROELECTRONICS INDUSTRY SUPPORT PROGRAMME

Assistance can be given, on a selective basis, to promote investment in the manufacture of microelectronic components and to encourage research and development of both product and processes.

All firms engaged in the manufacture of microelectronic components and those firms supplying specialised equipment, materials and services to the industry may be eligible. In order to qualify, research and development projects must cost a minimum of £25,000 although special consideration will be given to smaller projects where firms of groups employ less than 200 people.

In addition, it must be shown that:

(a) The company is viable, and has the technical and financial capability to carry through the project.

(b) The project must have a good prospect of success and significantly improve the company's performance.

(c) The project could not take place at all, or within a reasonable time-scale, without the government support.

A grant of up to 25% of qualifying costs for research and development and investment in production facilities is available. In the case of research and development projects, support is available in the form of a shared-cost contract of up to 50% of total qualifying project costs, recoverable by a levy on related sales.

Applications for assistance must be made before a project is started.

Further information Details are obtainable from:

Department of Trade and Industry,
Electronics Applications Division,
Kingsgate House,
66-74 Victoria St,
London SW1E 6SW
Tel: (01) 215 8002

MICROELECTRONICS APPLICATION PROJECT

The aim of this project is to encourage UK industry to apply microprocessor technology to a wide range of products and production processes.

Selective assistance is available to all sectors of UK manufacturing industry in the following ways.

Industrial training and awareness

The Department of Trade and Industry will assist with the cost of developing courses designed to train engineers in the use of microelectronics. The rate of grant will usually be 50% of allowable cost for public courses, 25% for in-house courses.

Feasibility studies and consultancy support

Grants of up to £3,000 are available towards the cost of consultancy work looking at the possibility of utilising microelectronics in products or production processes.

Development

The development costs, to commercial production of new or significantly improved products, may be eligible for a grant of up to 25% of qualifying costs (e.g., hardware and software trial installations, licensing and consultancy fees), or in exceptional cases, a shared cost contract of up to 50%.

To be eligible for any of the above, the company must be able to demonstrate points (a), (b) and (c) above, as in the microelectronics industry support programme.

Further information This is available from:

Department of Industry,
Electronics Applications Division,
Kingsgate House,
66-74 Victoria St,
London SW1E 6SW
Tel: (01) 215 8002

FLEXIBLE MANUFACTURING SYSTEMS

Flexible manufacturing is a system which combines microelectronics and mechanical engineering to bring economies of scale to batch work. A central on-line computer controls machine tools and other work stations and other components and tooling while also providing monitoring and information control. This combination of flexibility and overall control makes possible the production of a wide range of products in small numbers.

Grants are available to companies operating within the UK and which come within Division 3 of the 1980 Standard Industrial Classification. Assistance is given on a selective basis and in assessing the projects the Department of Trade and Industry will take into consideration:

* The viability of the company and the project.
* The degree of innovation in both the system and in the project's contribution to the whole manufacturing process.
* Whether the project introduces flexible manufacturing to a new sector of industry, or a new area of the country.
* Whether the project will act as a stimulus to the supply industry.
* Whether assistance would speed up the introduction of the project.

Grants of 50% of professional consultancy fees are available up to a maximum of £50,000. The consultants must be approved by the Department of Trade and Industry.

Grants of up to 25% are available towards development and capital costs, minimum expenditure £200,000.

Further information This is available from:

Department of Trade and Industry,
Mechanical Engineering and
Manufacturing Technology Division,
Ashdown House,
123 Victoria St,
London SW1E 6RB
Tel: (01) 212 0833

INDUSTRIAL ROBOT SUPPORT PROGRAMME

All manufacturing companies are eligible for selective assistance, and in exceptional circumstances non-manufacturing operations may be given support, in one of the following categories:

Consultancy support

25% of the cost of feasibility studies undertaken by independent consultants to establish whether robots can make an economic contribution to the product processes. The study may last up to 15 man-days.

Application

The capital and development costs associated with installing an industrial robot may attract a grant of up to 25%. The minimum project cost is £25,000, although smaller schemes may be considered.

Manufacture

A grant of up to 20% of qualifying costs is available to UK manufacturers of new industrial robot towards development and capital costs for projects involving design and development. The qualifying costs may include such things as the design and development of prototypes, trials, modifications and launching. Assistance is available for placing the newly designed robots with users for evaluation on the same basis as under the Support for Innovation Scheme.

Further information This is available from:

Department of Trade and Industry,
Mechanical Engineering and
Manufacturing Technology Division,
Room 520,
Ashdown House,
123 Victoria St,
London SW1E 6RB
Tel: (01) 212 0724

FIBRE-OPTIC AND OPTO-ELECTRONICS SCHEME

All firms involved in the design, development and application of products and processes related to optical fibres, opto-electronics, optical sensors and instruments required for these activities, can apply for support under this scheme.

Development

A grant of 25% is available towards the cost of research and development, similar to that available under the Support for Innovation Scheme. A shared-cost contract of up to 50% may be offered in exceptional circumstances. The minimum qualifying cost must be £25,000.

Application

A grant of 25% of a pre-production order is available for developing novel applications of fibre-optics and opto-electronic technology. Criteria of eligibility are the same as under the Support for Innovation Scheme.

Manufacture

Capital investment projects can attract a grant towards the cost of buildings, plant and equipment. The minimum project cost should normally be at least £500,000.

Further information This is available from:

Department of Trade and Industry,
Electronics Applications Division,
Kingsgate House,
66-74 Victoria St,
London SW1E 6SW
Tel: (01) 215 8002

BIOTECHNOLOGY SCHEME

This scheme is aimed at promoting investment in biotechnology research and development projects. The industries involved in this sector are food, agriculture, pharmaceuticals, chemicals, waste-treatment, mining, process plant and control equipment, scientific equipment and reagents, horticulture and oil.

Consultancy support

Feasibility studies into specific process and product developments, and markets, can attract a grant of up to 25% of project costs (to a project limit of £2,500).

Strategic studies to assess the commercial opportunities and risks presented by biotechnology may be eligible for grants of up to 50%, maximum grant £25,000.

Innovation grants

A grant of up to 25% towards support for research and development of innovative projects and processes, including demonstration projects, is available.

Further information This is available from:

Department of Trade and Industry,
Biotechnology Unit,
Cornwall House,
Waterloo Rd,
London SE1 8XY
Tel: (01) 211 8442

16 Other forms of assistance

NATIONAL SELECTIVE ASSISTANCE

Selective assistance under s. 8 of the Industrial Development Act 1982 is available throughout the UK (including the assisted areas) for major projects which are in the national interest. Assisted projects should normally involve new investment of at least £500,000 including working capital and ancillary costs associated with the new project. Assistance is provided on a selective basis and directed towards the manufacturing industry. Consideration will be given for commercial viable projects:

(a) where there is a genuine choice of international location;

(b) which will lead to substantial improvements in performance, usually productivity although other improvements such as quality or reliability of products will be considered;

(c) which will lead to the introduction of new products to the business;

(d) which will produce a substantial net contribution to UK output or will be a means of import substitution.

As with selective assistance under s. 7 of the Industrial Development Act, aid will only be given for projects that would not go ahead as proposed without aid. This means that there must be a genuine and significant enhancement of the project as a result of the assistance (additionality).

The assistance provided will be *negotiated* as the minimum necessary to allow the project to succeed. Usually it will be provided in the form of a cash grant payable over the length of the project, payment being made in instalments.

Further information This is available from:

Industrial Financial Appraisal Division,
Department of Trade and Industry,
Room 527,
Bridge Place,
88-89 Eccleston Square,
London SW1V 1PT
Tel: (01) 212 4150

The Scottish Economic Planning Department
Tel: (041) 248 2855

Welsh Office Industry Department
Tel: (0222) 825111

COAL FIRING SCHEMES

This assistance is to encourage commercial undertakings in the manufacturing industry, agriculture and certain service industries (excluding banking and insurance) to switch industrial equipment from oil and/or gas to coal firing. Assistance is available in the UK and is discretionary in that the soundness of the proposal plus the additionality criterion will be taken into account.

The assistance will be by way of a capital grant of up to 25% of the net eligible cost of the project (i.e., net of VAT and of any applicable regional development grant or European Community grant).

The minimum expenditure limit is £15,000 and there is no maximum.

ECSC loans have been made available to cover 50% of the cost of the conversion scheme which is eligible for the above mentioned grant. The loans will only be for eight years with a four-year grace period on the repayment of capital. Exchange risk guarantee scheme cover is also available. The borrowing limits for ECSC loans are minimum £15,000 and maximum £2 million.

Further information This can be obtained from:

Department of Energy,
Coal Firing Unit,
Thames House South,
Millbank,
London SW1P 4QJ
Tel: (01) 211 3743

In Northern Ireland information is available from:

Department of Economic Development,
Energy Division,
Massey Avenue
Belfast BT4 2JP

SMALL ENGINEERING FIRMS INVESTMENT SCHEME

This scheme was introduced on 30 March 1982 to make available to engineering firms employing less than 200 people a third of the investment cost of certain types of advanced capital equipment. The initial scheme was very successful in that the allocation of funds was quickly taken up and in March 1983 a further £100 million pounds was allocated to this scheme.

Further information This is available from Department of Trade and Industry regional offices.

SMALL FIRMS SERVICE

The small firms service is designed to help owners and managers of small businesses with their plans and problems. It acts as an advisory service to those people thinking of starting their own businesses as well as to people who are currently in business.

In general small firms can be considered for help, and the criterion is employing less than 200 persons. Information is free but for further counselling after the initial free meeting a modest fee is charged for each subsequent session. A wide range of business information and management advice and help can be given.

Further information This can be obtained by contacting the Regional Small Firms Centre (Tel: Freefone 2444).

BUSINESS EXPANSION SCHEME

The aim of this scheme is to encourage investment in new, small business by means of income tax incentives. The incentives are given to outside investors, rather than a person putting money into his or her own business.

The scheme includes almost all manufacturing, construction and service industries, including the retail and wholesale trades. The main exclusions are those companies involved in financial services, overseas companies, and subsidiaries.

The normal minimum investment by any investor in any one company is £500, and to qualify for full relief the capital must be invested for a period of at least five years. Relief is given at the investor's top rate of tax. (Each individual's maximum total investment qualifying for relief is currently £40,000.)

Under the terms of this scheme a person closely connected with the company cannot qualify for relief, i.e., if he or she:

(a) owns more than 30% of the ordinary shares;
(b) is a paid director; or
(c) is a partner or employee.

For these purposes, along with a person's own shares and interests, those of husband and wife, grandparents, parents, children or grandchildren are counted. Relief is available if the investment is in a company controlled by a sister or brother, nephew or niece, or more distant relatives.

These are only very broad outlines of the scheme, and before investing appropriate professional advice should be obtained to ensure that relief is applicable.

Further information This is available from:

Board of Inland Revenue,
Press Office,
Somerset House,
Strand,
London WC2R 1LB

LOAN GUARANTEES FOR SMALL BUSINESSES

The details of the Small Business Loan Guarantee Scheme were given in Part 1 (pp. 10-12).

Applications for the Loan Guarantee Scheme should be made to the firm's bankers.

Further information This is available from:

Department of Trade and Industry,
Loan Guarantee Unit,
Room 221,
Steel House,
11 Tothill St,
London SW1H 9NF
Tel: (01) 213 4719/3858/5358

THE ENTERPRISE ALLOWANCE

Often people starting up in business who have previously been unemployed, lose their regular income in the form of unemployment or supplementary benefit. An allowance of £40 per week for up to one year can be paid to individuals who:

(a) are between 18 and pensionable age;
(b) have been unemployed or under notice of redundancy for 13 weeks;
(c) have been receiving supplementary or unemployment benefit;
(d) can show that they have £1,000 which they intend to invest in a new business;
(e) will be working full-time in the new business.

Until recently this scheme has been operated in a few pilot areas, but it has now been extended to cover the whole country.

Further information This can be obtained from the local Job Centre.

INDUSTRIAL AND COMMERCIAL FINANCE CORPORATION

The ICFC is part of Investors in Industry (3i) which is owned by the major Scottish and English clearing banks and the Bank of England. It is an independent company which raises its funds from the private sector and lends to small and medium sized companies throughout the UK. It is one of the largest sources of finance for these businesses.

ICFC provides finance in a variety of forms and tailors every package to meet the individual requirements of the applicants. It can provide loans, subscribe for or purchase shares, assist with hire-purchase, leasing and guarantees.

It offers finance for business start-up schemes as well as expansion projects and may seek a minority share in the equity of a new company (although it rarely interferes in the running of the business).

Loan repayments are normally between 5 and 20 year at competitive rates of interest. The rate is fixed at the beginning of the loan and interest charged on the outstanding balance.

The ICFC is an agent for the European Investment Bank, The European Commission and the European Coal and Steel Community, and is able to make funds available to small firms under the relevant schemes. The amounts available range from £15,000 to £250,000 and can represent up to 50% of the capital expenditure on any project. To qualify companies must be in the manufacturing, selected service or tourist industries. Within the assisted areas (see p. 160-177), the upper limit for loans is £2 million.

The European loans can be given at an interest rate below the market rate, and capital repayments may be deferred for the first two years.

Further information Enquiries should be addressed to any of the ICFC's area offices, or:

ICFC
91 Waterloo Rd
London SE1 8XP
Tel: (01) 928 7822

INDUSTRIAL COMMON OWNERSHIP MOVEMENT

The Industrial Common Ownership Movement offers finance to new and expanding worker cooperatives through Industrial Common Ownership Finance Ltd.

There are no set limits for the loans, but loans of less than £1,000 are not usually given, and the average range is £5,000 to £15,000. Loans are made for periods of up to five years at slightly less than commercial rates, and security is normally required.

Further information This is available from:

Industrial Common Ownership Finance Ltd,
4 St Giles St,
Northampton NN1 1AA
Tel: (0604) 37563

GRANTS FROM EUROPE FOR SMALL FIRMS — BUSINESS IMPROVEMENT SERVICES

As from 1985 the European Regional Development Fund and the Department of Trade and Industry are offering grants in areas affected by job losses in steel, shipbuilding and textile industries to help new businesses start up and existing small firms to grow. A total of £63 million is available and open to applicants until December 1988 — dependent on uptake of funds.

If firms are:

(a) setting up in business;

(b) an independent small firm employing up to 200 people, or part of a group employing that number;

(c) a consultant, or any other kind of organisation, providing or intending to provide a service to small firms;

then they should look at the package of grants.

It must be remembered that these grants are to help small firms in specific geographical areas.

Where the grants are available

Steel areas

Cleveland
Corby TTWA
Assisted areas in Durham (including parts of Consett TTWA located in Northumberland and Tyne and Wear)
Assisted areas in Humberside (including parts of Scunthorpe TTWA located in Lincolnshire)
South Yorkshire (including Sheffield TTWA)
Workington TTWA

Shipbuilding areas

Cleveland
Tyne and Wear
Merseyside

Textiles areas

In West Yorkshire:
- Bradford TTWA
- Dewsbury TTWA
- Halifax TTWA
- Huddersfield TTWA
- Keighley TTWA
- Todmorden TTWA

In Lancashire:
- Accrington TTWA
- Blackburn TTWA
- Burnley TTWA
- Lancaster TTWA
- Nelson TTWA
- Rossendale TTWA

In Greater Manchester:
- Ashton under Lyne TTWA
- Bolton TTWA
- Bury TTWA
- Leigh TTWA
- Oldham TTWA
- Rochdale TTWA
- Wigan TTWA

TTWA = Travel-to-Work Area, as defined on 1 February 1984 by the Department of Employment.

All manufacturing activities qualify for grant except the textile, steel and shipbuilding industries (unless they are diversifying into new activities). Most of the service sector is also eligible. But certain activities, like retailing and personal services, do not qualify.

Growth and development

Business Improvement Services can help a small firm with most stages of growth and development, from identifying new products, through market research and consultancy advice, to the purchase of fixed assets. Help can also be given with the provision of common services for groups of small firms.

Some grants are paid direct to the small firms, some to the provider of the service.

* 55% grants towards the cost of a general *business check-up* to establish key areas for improvement and possibly identify the need for specific follow-up consultancy works. Maximum grant £500.

Marketing

* 55% grants towards the cost of a review of a firm's current marketing activities and the drawing up of a *marketing strategy* for the future. Maximum grant £1,500 in England, £1,000 in Wales.

* 70% grants towards the cost of *market research studies* to explore the market potential — regional, national or export — for new and existing products, processes and services. Maximum grant £7,000 for overseas markets, £3,500 for domestic markets.

* 55% grants towards the cost of *translations* of market information and sales literature from or into foreign languages. Maximum grant £1,500 in England, £1,000 in Wales.

Management and financial advice

* 55% grants towards the cost of advice on improving your existing *budget and control systems*, or the installation and operation of a new financial management system. Maximum grant £2,500 (restricted to £500 if company has previously received budget and control advice), £1,000 Wales.

* 55% grants towards the cost of *business plan* and *financial restructuring* advice.

New products and processes

* 70% grants towards the cost of *feasibility projects* leading to the development of new products and processes. The work can be done in-house or by outside consultants. Maximum grant normally £35,000.

* 55% grants towards the cost of *licensing in* a new product, process or item of technology. A consultant can be employed to help identify several propositions, evaluate them and then negotiate a deal with the licensor. Maximum grant £5,500.

* 55% grants towards the cost of *translations* can also cover technical documents, specifications, standards and legislative requirements.

Computer applications service

* 55% grants towards the cost of investigating the merits of acquiring a microcomputer, and associated software packages, to meet the needs of the business. Maximum grant £1,500 England, £1,000 Wales.

Other consultancy work

* BIS offers grants for a range of consultancy advice. If a business needs consultancy advice in an area not already described in this section, this may be eligible for a 55% grant up to a maximum of £1,500 in England and £1,000 in Wales.

Common services

* 55% grants towards the operating costs of a *group* of small firms in joining together to take advantage of common services, including typing, duplicating, book-keeping, word processors, or microcomputers. Grant will cover a maximum three-year period.

Investment projects

* 20% grants towards the cost of fixed assets, including plant, buildings and machinery. Maximum grant £20,000. These grants are only available for firms with up to *25 employees*. The need for such investment must have been identified as a result of market research or other studies. (Projects are not also eligible for discretionary assistance under s. 7 of the Industrial Development Act 1982, but in appropriate areas, regional development grants may be claimed.)

Providers of services

If a business *provides services* to small firms in the eligible areas, BIS can help with:

* 70% grants towards the cost of *market research* studies to help *groups* of small firms exploit the market potential — regional, national or export — for new and existing products, processes and services. Maximum grant £7,000 for overseas markets, £2,500 for domestic markets.

* 70% grants towards the cost of *risk appraisal* work done by or for providers of small-scale equity investment to one or more small firms. Maximum grant normally £1,500.

* 55% grants towards the cost of providing *common services* to a group of small firms. Grants can cover a maximum three-year period.

* 55% grants towards the cost of new *advisory and counselling services* for small firms in eligible areas. Where the applicant is an existing organisation, grant will only be offered on an extension of services into new activities. Grants can cover a maximum three-year period.

* 55% grants towards the cost of providing information relating to product and technological innovation to small firms through *databases* and other services. Databases need not be computerised. Grants can cover a maximum three-year period.

* 50% towards the cost of employing *enterprise personnel* to promote the assistance available for small firms, including grants under BIS and to encourage and help firms to take advantage of it. Grants can cover a maximum four-year period.

Providers can be from the private sector, local enterprise agencies, chambers of commerce, large firms interested in helping small firms, or local authorities, depending on the service. A firm interested in providing new services for small firms in eligible areas, should approach the Department of Trade and Industry's Regional Office.

There is no limit to the number of services which can be applied for. The Department may restrict the total amount of grant help which they give to any one firm or organisation.

Depending upon the take-up of funds, applications will be accepted up to 25 November 1990. Grants will not be paid on work carried out after 25 February 1991.

Further information This can be obtained from the local Department of Trade and Industry office:

Department of Trade and Industry: Enquiry points for BIS

North-Eastern region:
Stanegate House,
2 Groat Market,
Newcastle upon Tyne NE1 1YN
Tel: (091) 232 4722 ext. 230

North-Western region:
Sunley Tower,
Piccadilly Plaza,
Manchester M1 4BA
Tel: (061) 236 2171 ext. 513

Merseyside sub-office:
Graeme House,
Derby Square,
Liverpool L2 7UP
Tel: (051) 227 4111 ext. 463

Yorkshire and Humberside region:
Priestley House,
3-5 Park Row,
Leeds LS1 5LF
Tel: (0532) 443171 ext. 229

East Midlands region:
Severns House,
20 Middle Pavement,
Nottingham NG1 7DW
Tel: (0602) 506181 ext. 358

Index